Comments on other *Amazing Stories* from readers & reviewers

"Tightly written volumes filled with lots of wit and humour about famous and infamous Canadians."
Eric Shackleton, *The Globe and Mail*

"The heightened sense of drama and intrigue, combined with a good dose of human interest is what sets Amazing Stories *apart."*
Pamela Klaffke, *Calgary Herald*

"This is popular history as it should be... For this price, buy two and give one to a friend."
Terry Cook, a reader from Ottawa, on **Rebel Women**

"Glasner creates the moment of the explosion itself in graphic detail...she builds detail upon gruesome detail to create a convincingly authentic picture."
Peggy McKinnon, *The Sunday Herald*, on **The Halifax Explosion**

"It was wonderful...I found I could not put it down. I was sorry when it was completed."
Dorothy F. from Manitoba on **Marie-Anne Lagimodière**

"Stories are rich in description, and bristle with a clever, stylish realness."
Mark Weber, *Central Alberta Advisor*, on **Ghost Town Stories II**

"A compelling read. Bertin...has selected only the most intriguing tales, which she narrates with a wealth of detail."
Joyce Glasner, *New Brunswick Reader*, on **Strange Events**

"The resulting book is one readers will want to share with all the women in their lives."
Lynn Martel, *Rocky Mountain Outlook*, on **Women Explorers**

RENÉ LÉVESQUE

AMAZING STORIES®

RENÉ LÉVESQUE
The Fascinating Life
of a Separatist Icon

BIOGRAPHY

by Megan Durnford

PUBLISHED BY ALTITUDE PUBLISHING CANADA LTD.
1500 Railway Avenue, Canmore, Alberta T1W 1P6
www.altitudepublishing.com
www.amazingstories.ca
1-800-957-6888

Extreme care has been taken to ensure that all information presented in
this book is accurate and up to date. Neither the author nor the
publisher can be held responsible for any errors.

Publisher	Stephen Hutchings
Associate Publisher	Kara Turner
Editors	Frances Purslow & Dianne Smyth
Digital Photo Colouring	Bryan Pezzi

We acknowledge the financial support of the Government
of Canada through the Book Publishing Industry Development
Program (BPIDP) for our publishing activities.

Altitude GreenTree Program
Altitude Publishing will plant twice as many trees as were used
in the manufacturing of this product.

National Library of Canada Cataloguing in Publication Data

Durnford, Megan
    Rene Levesque / Megan Durnford.

(Amazing stories)
ISBN 1-55439-058-3

1. Lévesque, René, 1922-1987. 2. Québec (Province)--History-
Autonomy and independence movements. 3. Quebec (Province)-
Politics and government--1976-1985. 4. Parti québecois--Biography.
5. Prime ministers--Québec (Province)--Biography. I. Title.
II. Series: Amazing stories (Calgary, Alta.)

FC2925.1.L5D87 2005   971.4'04'092   C2005-905229-5

Amazing Stories® is a registered trademark of Altitude Publishing Canada Ltd.

Printed and bound in Canada by Friesens
2 4 6 8 9 7 5 3 1

To everyone who is pursuing a dream.
To my husband, Laurent Dionne,
for his constant love and support.
And to my mother, Nancy Durnford-Lorimer,
one of the strongest women I know.

Contents

Prologue 11

Chapter 1 Frolicking between Forest and Coast 13

Chapter 2 Lévesque in Uniform 22

Chapter 3 Radio-Canada's Rising Star 31

Chapter 4 The Nationalization Hero 46

Chapter 5 Birth of a Separatist 60

Chapter 6 Growing Pains 74

Chapter 7 The PQ — A Serious Political Contender . . 86

Chapter 8 Premier René Lévesque 100

Chapter 9 Reshaping Quebec Society 109

Chapter 10 The End of a Dream 118

Prologue

Thousands of people gathered at the Paul Sauvé Arena in east end Montreal. They chanted, clapped, and waved fleur-de-lis flags. The crowd was united by an electrifying sense of joy.

The impossible had happened. The Parti Québécois (PQ), a new political party that promised Quebeckers a chance to build their own nation, had just won the November 1976 election. René Lévesque, the driving force behind this dream, was the new premier of Quebec.

A group of students began to sing Gilles Vigneault's nationalist refrain: "Gens du pays, c'est votre tour, de vous laisser parler d'amour..." *Then, one by one, more people joined in until the entire sports centre resonated with the sound of more than 5000 voices. Some people were so delirious with happiness that they spontaneously hugged complete strangers.*

René Lévesque had just finished a rousing speech at the Taillon riding headquarters and he was on his way to Paul Sauvé Arena with a police escort. He had hoped that the Parti Québécois would win a few more seats than during the last provincial election, but he had never imagined that the PQ would form a majority government. Lévesque was still in shock from the sudden victory.

Lévesque entered the arena to thunderous applause. Quebeckers were incredibly proud of this charismatic

Gaspésien. *As he attempted to make his way to the stage, supporters tried to embrace him, congratulate him, or merely touch him.*

Finally, Lévesque reached the stage and walked towards the microphone. People cheered and chanted so loudly that it was almost deafening. Lévesque motioned with his hands for quiet — and he began to speak ...

Chapter 1
Frolicking between Forest and Coast

oung René Lévesque looked up from the book he was reading, to gaze out of his bedroom window. Across the dark blue water of the Baie des Chaleurs he could see the red cliffs of Paspébiac, a neighbouring village. Lévesque and his friends had a lot of fun in Paspébiac, lolling around in a lagoon that was sheltered by a sandbar. The boys would float and dream in the warm, almost tropical, water for hours.

Lévesque had seen the whitewashed buildings of Robin, Jones and Whitman Ltd. fisheries at Paspébiac, but he didn't know that the French-speaking fishermen who brought in the cod for the Anglophone company were pawns in a feudal system. He didn't know that the fishermen were underpaid, or that the pay was not in dollars, but in "chips," that could only be used at food and clothing stores owned by the same company. The Paspébiac fisheries operation was characteristic of Quebec society in the 1920s — a minority English-speaking population controlled the economy — while the French-Canadian majority comprised the labour force.

The young René Lévesque was unaware of the exploitation of the fishermen, just as he was unaware that one day his leadership would enable Quebeckers to take control of their own destiny.

In an interesting twist of fate, Quebec's most celebrated nationalist was not born in the province of Quebec. Shortly after their marriage in 1920, Lévesque's parents, Dominique and Diane, left a privileged life in Rivière-du-Loup, for the village of New Carlisle on the Gaspé peninsula, so that Dominique, who was a young lawyer, could take on greater professional challenges. Dominique had accepted work as an assistant to a prominent Irish-Canadian lawyer and entrepreneur, John Hall Kelly, until he was in a position to open his own legal firm. Moving to New Carlisle was quite difficult for Lévesque's mother. In Rivière-du-Loup she had had every creature comfort. In New Carlisle, their first house did not even have running water.

When Diane went into labour with their first child, a doctor was summoned to the Lévesque home. The incompetent (and possibly drunk) doctor who attended the delivery of this child accidentally broke the baby's neck with his forceps.

The baby died shortly after birth. When Diane discovered that she was pregnant again, she vowed that she would give birth to their second child in a hospital. In 1922, the closest hospital to New Carlisle was in the town of Campbelltown, across the Baie des Chaleurs. On August 24, René (which means "born again") came into this world in Campbelltown, New Brunswick.

Apart from a case of jaundice when he was newborn, René was a healthy baby boy. He was sweet, smart, and mischievous. His fantastic sense of curiosity, which would serve him well in his future journalism career, caused his mother no end of grief when he was a toddler. One summer, after René set fire to a fence, his mother tethered his ankle to the back porch railing to prevent him from causing more damage.

John Kelly was asked to be René's godfather. The millionaire entrepreneur, who lived in a baroque-style castle at the entrance to the village, gave the Lévesque family a rattan baby carriage, but never took the godfather role seriously. Far from feeling honoured by this spiritual duty, Kelly was likely resentful that his employee had made this request.

Over the next few years, René's siblings, Fernand, André, and Alice, arrived on the scene. Although René was sometimes protective of his sister Alice, he was a bit of a brat. Alice recalled that there were always a lot of arguments when the children played croquet. René insisted on leading the game and he was a poor loser. If André sensed that he was going to win a round, he would start to run away right after the winning strike. He knew that his oldest brother, René, would chase after him.

René's parents sometimes put the little rascal on a train to Rivière-du-Loup, where he stayed with his maternal grandparents. Far from resenting these forced holidays, René kept busy with amusing tasks, such as minding the candy counter at his grandparents' general store and filling in for *grandmaman*'s friends at card games. Grandmaman set up her grandson with sufficient risk capital and then taught him the rules of bridge and poker.

New Carlisle, a genteel town on the north shore of the Baie des Chaleurs, looked like it had been transplanted from New England. Its tree-lined streets, grand Loyalist heritage homes, and Protestant churches were an anomaly on the Gaspé peninsula.

Most of the French-speaking people who lived in this region were poor fishermen. The Lévesque family was one of the few bourgeois French-speaking families in town because Dominique was a lawyer. When René was three years old, his father bought a large, white wooden house with a lovely portico and a view onto the Baie des Chaleurs. The Lévesque family also bought one of the first automobiles in town. As well, they had the means to erect a radio antenna so that they could receive broadcasts from CKAC, the first French radio station in North America.

Left to their own devices much of the time, René and his friends grew up frolicking between the forest and the coast. In a scene that is hard to imagine today, the young boys taught each other how to swim. They went to a local beach and took turns diving off a dock. One of the boys was stationed in the water to save anyone who was spluttering too much and liable to drown.

When René was at home, he spent a lot of time with his father learning about French literature and culture. He learned to read by looking at Jean de la Fontaine fables while sitting on his father's lap. A few years later, father and son perused the *Montreal Standard* newspaper supplement together. They laughed at the comics and then settled down to a battle of wits with the crossword puzzle. Although Dominique's English accent was atrocious, his English vocabulary was impressive because most of his clients at the law firm were English-speaking.

The Lévesque home was jam-packed with reading material. Young René soon began to read a great variety of books, including science fiction by Jules Verne and other adventure stories that had been sanctioned by the local Catholic censor. Then René discovered that the family library also contained more risqué stories, such as *The Flapper*.

Lévesque learned far more about reading and writing at home than he did at the local one-room schoolhouse. At the schoolhouse, there were around 50 children, at different scholastic levels, from both English- and French-speaking families. This made it difficult for some to pay attention. The children did learn new words in each other's language in the classroom, but they learned even more during snowball fights, tag, and other childhood games. They sometimes exchanged barbs, such as "French pea soup" and "English crayfish," but no malice was intended. Language was not an issue for the children.

The Baie des Chaleurs area was settled by two sets of dispossessed peoples, French-speaking Acadians and English-speaking Loyalists. In the late-1700s, following the Acadian expulsion from the Maritime provinces, French-speaking Acadians began to settle around the Baie des Chaleurs due to its bounty of fish. As of 1783, when Great Britain recognized U.S. independence, American citizens who were loyal to the British crown fled to Canada. A group of Loyalists established the town of New Carlisle.

There was no French high school in New Carlisle, so René's parents decided to send their eldest son to study at a Jesuit seminary in the town of Gaspé, hundreds of kilometres from New Carlisle. René was one of the lucky ones. Most of the French-speaking children who lived on the Baie des Chaleurs didn't study past the primary grades, because their parents could not afford to send them to boarding school.

When René was dropped off at the Jesuit Séminaire de Gaspé, his first question was: "Where is the library?" As he began to look through the Jesuits' book collection, he was amazed to discover that he had already read most of them. Books were René's lifeline. After diligently completing his homework, he sometimes re-read *Histoire du Canada* and his other textbooks, for pleasure. Although he was the youngest boy in his class, René soon proved himself to be an excellent scholar.

Yet boarding school was a rude shock to René. Not only was he far away from his parents and his siblings, he was forced to adapt to a strict and regimented life with few creature comforts. The dormitory and classroom furnishings were spartan. And the food was extremely plain. For dinner, the nuns served up a variety of concoctions made from potatoes, water, onions, and flour, along with *fèves au lard* (beans cooked with pork). René was entitled to three eggs a week because his family could afford the supplement.

Recreation consisted of handball, hockey (after the boys had flooded and shovelled off the rink), and smoking. The boys did not need to smoke surreptitiously because the supervisors, nicotine addicts themselves, were resigned to the boys' tobacco habit.

René and his classmates quickly found ways to beat the system in order to make their forced stay at the seminary more amusing. For instance, on Saturday nights the boys were supposed to take baths, however, the water in the attic bath cubicles was frigid. So the clever boys began concealing books in their dressing gown pockets on their way to the baths; then they read while making splashing noises with one foot in the bath. The warders never suspected a thing as the boys sauntered downstairs in their fresh clothes, carrying wet towels.

René had his first taste of political discourse at the

seminary. When his young teachers returned to their families for holidays, many of them got caught up in the breeze of nationalist fervour. The Jesuits did not formally teach the children about aspirations to French-Canadian nationhood, however, it was pretty obvious where their sympathies lay. One of the most incendiary intellectuals of the day, Father Dubé (better known by his pseudonym, François Hertel) was the cousin of one of the seminary masters. This flamboyant writer who dared to envisage the separation of Quebec was ultimately defrocked for his provocative texts. As René was still just a boy who was trying to make friends and keep up his tennis game, much of the nationalist discussion was over his head.

Barely a year later, his carefree childhood came to a crashing halt. His father, Dominique, had been suffering from vague stomach pains. The doctors were convinced that he was suffering from appendicitis, so he was operated on in Campbelltown. During his post-surgical convalescence, Dominique began to deteriorate. This case was clearly beyond the abilities of the local physicians, so Dominique was promptly shipped off to Quebec City. René and his mother and younger siblings quickly left for Quebec City on the Ocean Express train. When they saw Diane's sister and brother waiting on the platform at Rivière-du-Loup, they knew that there was no need to continue their voyage to Quebec City. Dominique was dead at 48.

Dominique was Lévesque's first mentor and "the most

important man" in his life. Many decades after Dominique's death, Lévesque's second wife Corinne Côté said, "[René] had an unfinished history with his father … I think that it was the first shock in his life and that he never really recovered from the fact that he couldn't continue the very special relationship that he had with his father."

Chapter 2
Lévesque in Uniform

Following Dominique's sudden death, Lévesque's mother made two significant decisions that further destabilized his world: she decided to move her young family from the Anglo-dominated town of New Carlisle to Quebec City, and she married a friend of the family named Albert Pelletier.

In September 1938, Lévesque was enrolled at Collège Garnier, a Jesuit day school. Lévesque felt like a bit of a country bumpkin in the capital city. Shortly after his arrival at Garnier, he wrote in the student paper, "On September 6, a boy from the Gaspé who felt kind of nervous and like a fish out of water, arrived in Champlain's historic city. The poor boy wondered anxiously whether he would last a long time there."

He didn't feel awkward for very long. Lévesque was soon recognized as a brilliant scholar, especially in written and spoken French. His rhetoric professor also commented on Lévesque's special talent for improvised debate.

In Quebec City, Lévesque met Louise L'Heureux, daughter of the editor of the daily *L'Action Catholique*, while she was skating with friends. Lévesque wasn't especially interested in skating, but he was happy to escort the dark-haired beauty home afterward. He was smitten by this glamorous girl who shared his intellectual curiosity and libertine attitudes. Lévesque was also very interested in getting to know her erudite, nationalist father.

Lévesque was just 16 and he was hell-bent on enjoying all of Quebec City's pleasures: dancing, playing cards, boxing, chatting with friends, and watching the latest films. Sometimes, he just spent the evening cuddling and giggling with Louise.

Lévesque also began to work part-time as an announcer for CKCV, a local radio station. He was not new to radio. Back in New Carlisle, his father had recommended his eldest son to a dentist who operated a bilingual radio station (CHNC) as a hobby. During the summer after his father's death, Lévesque worked there translating news releases from English to French and vice versa. Whenever the regular announcer was ill, Lévesque had gone "on air."

Soon, the CKCV job and card games were taking up all of Lévesque's time and there was little time left to study. He later admitted to a friend that the tedium and limitations of boarding school had made it easier for him to focus on his schoolwork, so he never had mediocre marks. At Collège Garnier, his marks plummeted from exceptional to failing. After he received one percent on a math exam, the college rector suggested that Lévesque leave Garnier. He then wrote Lévesque a recommendation for a seminary that was well known for helping students who had gone off the rails.

Lévesque desperately missed his father, and he never really accepted his mother's remarriage. Lévesque had childhood memories of Monsieur Pelletier, a lawyer like his father, joining the Lévesque family for picnics and card games, and he did not relish Pelletier trying to step into his father's shoes. Lévesque ensured that he never felt indebted to Pelletier. Later in life, Lévesque told a reporter that he had been earning extra money at CKCV in order to help out his widowed mother. Yet, Pelletier was doing a fine job of supporting the Lévesque household in Quebec City.

Lévesque then decided to enter law school at Laval University, fulfilling one of his mother's most ardent desires. Diane had beamed when her young son announced that he was going to be a lawyer "like Papa." She was so convinced that her eldest son would take over Dominique's legal practice that she had not sold his old office. It was rented out in anticipation of Lévesque's return to New Carlisle.

Although he had the best of intentions when he began to study law, Lévesque was soon bored by the stodgy professors and the monotonous nature of legal studies. "Judge Roy delivered his course in Roman law in a tedious monotone, a course he had concocted a quarter of a century before and hadn't altered as much as a sigh since, like Roman law itself," he complained. Lévesque was also annoyed to discover that smoking was prohibited in class. When he continued to smoke anyway, he was summarily thrown out of class.

Lévesque began spending more time playing poker with his classmate Jean Marchand than attending classes. Slowly but surely, the reluctant law student realized that journalism was better suited to his character than law. He thoroughly enjoyed his part-time radio work — writing compelling reports and broadcasting the information with flair. So when his job at CKCV was terminated at the beginning of 1942, Lévesque approached CBV (the local Radio-Canada station). Due to the war effort, CBV was short-staffed, so the producers were interested in this dynamic, bilingual candidate. He was offered a one-month trial run. Lévesque was a hit. He was a terrific interviewer because he could "think on his feet," and he was also adept at reviewing literature and theatre because his classical education had provided him with a strong grounding in the liberal arts.

A short time later, the Canadian army contacted Lévesque about his requisite medical exam, and the abstract "news item" of conscription suddenly became more personal. Although Lévesque wanted to be a participant in this historic event, he was damned if he was going over in his majesty's uniform!

Lévesque decided that he would go to war as a journalist. While searching for a war correspondent position, Lévesque received an official expulsion notice from Laval University. The letter probably came as a relief.

There were no correspondent positions available with Radio-Canada. However, one of his colleagues told him that the American Office of War Information was looking for bilingual correspondents. The American army offered Lévesque an opportunity to go overseas as a member of the French language service of the Voice of America. When Lévesque was sent to New York City to meet the head of his department, he entered the flamboyant world of Pierre Lazareff. This spirited Jewish refugee, the former editor of the tabloid *Paris-Soir,* taught Lévesque everything he needed to know to help the Allied cause.

After basic training that winter in New York, Lévesque returned home to Quebec City. Then, one spring day he received a top-secret message. He had to cut all contact with his family and go to Montreal immediately, where he was expected to board *L'Indochinois.* The little freighter headed out to Europe on the foggy night of May 2,1944, with a disparate group of about 20 passengers, including American technicians, British children returning home, and the young journalist René Lévesque. Back in Quebec City, Louise l'Heureux already anxiously awaited the return of her fiancé.

London was so exciting that Lévesque actually forgot to report for duty right away! After years of admiring Trafalgar Square, London Bridge, and other British icons in magazines and books, Lévesque was simply amazed to be in the presence of these monuments. After two days of exploring London, Lévesque finally presented himself to the American Broadcasting Station in Europe (ABSIE). Lazareff was there barking orders and adding to the prevailing state of pandemonium. Lévesque's new colleagues seemed so non-plussed by his late arrival that he wished that he had spent more time playing tourist.

At ABSIE, Lévesque wrote and broadcast general news reports, commentaries, and updates on the progress of the war for a French-speaking audience. He later said, "I never had the impression that I was lying. But it was incredible the number of things that we didn't say."

On June 6, 1944, Lévesque learned that 150,000 Allied soldiers, supported by 3000 boats and thousands of planes, were storming the beaches of Normandy. The ABSIE employees knew that an operation of this magnitude was in the works, however they did not know the planned date. Sitting comfortably in his radio studio, Lévesque felt deeply troubled. Part of him envied the brave young men who were participating in a historic battle. On the other hand, Lévesque knew full well that thousands of soldiers would be slaughtered during this suicide mission. D-Day marked the beginning of the end of the Nazi Empire. One by one, French towns and cities were liberated. Lévesque followed the progress of the Allied forces in Paris with a small map that his father had given him a few years before his death.

René Lévesque

Now that it looked like the war was almost over, Lévesque was itching to cross the channel and have a look at Europe before he was sent home. In January 1945, he wrote to his family, "After three weeks in a training site, I am on the list of correspondents who are "leaving out." Where? I don't know and I don't care ... When? In 1945, I certainly hope."

A few weeks later, Lévesque began his new position as a liaison agent between the American army and the local population. He travelled in a tank with a group of young American soldiers through the battlefields and the decimated towns of eastern France and Germany. Most days, Lévesque would go for a little excursion around the area and then write a report on what he had seen. In the evenings, the tank crew washed down army rations with French wine, which had been "liberated" from abandoned homes.

The war was ending, but it was not over yet. So Lévesque and the rest of the crew were always on the lookout for Nazi guerrillas, known as Werwolves. They never met any Werwolves. However, they had a few close calls, including one with four young assassins in Nuremberg. Lévesque recalled in his memoirs —

Two grenades flew out of a basement window. One rolled harmlessly into the gutter, but the other smashed the front of one of our vehicles. A conditioned reflex sent us sprawling behind a wall. After two or three shots fired in the direction of the cellar, out came first a piece of rag more or less white, then four kids, three boys and a girl, in their *Hitlerjugend* outfits. The oldest wasn't fifteen. What could we do with these kindergarten assassins who could easily have finished us off? Each one of the dangerous prisoners was frisked, knocked around a little, and then requested, in English, French and unmistakable gestures, to get the hell out of there — *schnell!*

In May, Lévesque arrived at Dachau, the notorious concentration camp. He was deeply disturbed that some devout Bavarians had cheerfully pointed the way to Dachau with as much exhuberance as if they were indicating the way to the zoo. When the American contingent arrived at Dachau's main building with its sinister lookout towers and barbed wire fence, they began to look for the German garrison. The Nazi soldiers were on the run. They had left Dachau barely 15 minutes before.

Lévesque noticed rail cars that were sitting idle on the tracks. Through an opening, he could see rotting corpses hanging like animal carcasses. He stood transfixed. Suddenly, out of nowhere, hundreds of skeletal figures in striped pyjamas ran towards the soldiers, hysterical with relief. The American soldiers made their way around the former killing factory in stunned silence. Then the former inmates formed a circle and began to shout. They had located a *kapo*, (former inmate who had collaborated with the Germans) who had been hiding. One skeletal prisoner, gaining tremendous strength from revenge, beat the kapo into a bloody pulp.

Nauseated from the fetid odour of burning flesh and shocked to his very core, the young Canadian journalist could barely focus his thoughts long enough to describe this hell on earth.

Chapter 3
Radio-Canada's Rising Star

hen World War II ended, René Lévesque was shipped back to North America on a crowded boat with 12,000 other soldiers. Although Lévesque had only been away from Quebec for about 18 months, the province that Lévesque returned to was different than the one that he had left. Traditional rural society had already started to change in Quebec at the beginning of the century, due to modern industrialization. World War II accelerated the pace of this transformation. During the war, thousands of Quebec men left the calm of their conservative and isolated society to fight in Europe. And thousands of Quebec women abandoned their conventional domestic roles to work in factories. Traditional Quebec society was further changed by revolutionary legislation

introduced in the early 1940s by the Liberal Godbout government — compulsory education for children under the age of
14 — and voting rights for women.

René was 23 years old and ready for his next adventure
when he was offered a position at Radio-Canada's French-language international service in Montreal — La Voix du Canada
(the voice of Canada) — which broadcast Canadian news and
cultural reports to French-speaking audiences around the
world. It wasn't a very glamorous job and Lévesque certainly
was not well paid, but he was honing his journalistic skills
and he was getting to know a brilliant and erudite director
named Judith Jasmin. Lévesque was immediately attracted to
Jasmin's keen insights and her high journalistic standards.

Lévesque was an excellent announcer, although his
odd voice was a cause for concern. While working overseas,
Lévesque had contracted a bad case of laryngitis. The infection
was not properly treated, and his voice remained hoarse and
raspy thereafter.

When he wasn't on air, Lévesque enjoyed discover-
ing Montreal's cinemas, bookstores, restaurants, and other
cosmopolitan pleasures. Post-war Montreal was a pleasure
palace. Lévesque was disinclined to visit Quebec City on
weekends, despite repeated urging from his mother and
his fiancée. This was in part because he found Quebec City
parochial after living in London for a year. Lévesque was also
reluctant to deal with Diane and Louise's demands.

Lévesque's mother was still talking about law school.

As resolute as a dog with a bone, Diane could not relinquish her career aspirations for her eldest son. Lévesque and his mother had always had an awkward love-hate relationship because their personalities were so similar; both mother and son were inquisitive, hotheaded, and impulsive. And they could both be incredibly stubborn. Even after Lévesque had been premier for two years, Diane lamented, "Poor little boy, I feel sorry for you. Politics is so cruel and so uncertain. Ah! If you'd only finished your law school!"

Meanwhile, Louise l'Heureux, who had waited patiently for Lévesque to return from overseas, was keen to get married. René wanted to honour his commitment — a gentleman's duty — yet he no longer felt the same way about Louise as he had before going overseas. The spark was gone. Also, due to his wartime experience, Lévesque felt that he was no longer the same man who had proposed marriage to Louise. In a letter dated February 1947, Lévesque revealed to a friend, "The world seems to be upside-down and my place in the world is not clear to me. This past year has been filled with 'if,' 'but,' and 'maybe.'"

Nevertheless, René and Louise were married in Quebec City on May 3, 1947. After a traditional wedding, the newly-weds took the train to Virginia Beach. The dutiful son did not stop his regular correspondence just because he was on his honeymoon. He sent his mother postcards from New York City and the coast —

"Hello Mom! You see how much we are travelling — two days and we have already changed hotels! The one that you can see at the top of the page is magnificent — and it costs a fortune … I am sitting at a hand-embossed table with bronze desk accessories. The sun is wonderful, so is the beach. I am already tanned."

Upon their return to Montreal, Louise and René moved about a half-dozen times before they finally settled into their new home, 3355 Barclay Avenue, one week before Christmas. In the spring, Lévesque became a proud papa. Although he appreciated the simple pleasures of fatherhood and was fascinated by baby Pierre's gurgles and chuckles, he did not make any concessions for family life. He took on every reporting assignment that came along, even those that involved being away from home for days at a time.

In the summer of 1949, Lévesque's excellent reporting landed him an assignment for Radio-Canada's domestic service. This show, called *Journalistes au micro*, involved interviewing journalists about the day's top stories and about their professional lives. Amid the clinking of glasses and the din of conversation at the Laurentian Hotel, Lévesque engaged four journalists in a fascinating conversation. The public lapped it up.

When their second child, Claude, was born in 1950, Lévesque was briefly preoccupied with household concerns, such as washing dishes and running errands to the pharmacy. But he did not find domestic bliss gratifying for very long.

Lévesque was absolutely enthralled by his journalism career. When *Journalistes au micro* was discontinued, despite rave reviews, Lévesque was very disappointed. However, a much bigger journalistic opportunity was already on the horizon.

In June 1950, five divisions of the North Korean army supported by 300,000 Chinese soldiers crossed the border into South Korea and provoked a nasty civil war. The American army stepped into the mess in order to help liberate South Korea. Lévesque was familiar with the issues involved in the Korean War, due to his Radio-Canada International experience. When he realized that not many of his colleagues were interested in going to Korea, Lévesque "enthusiastically volunteered for the job," according to a Radio-Canada document. In 1951, he was sent to Korea for six months. There, Lévesque joined a battalion of the Royal Canadian Regiment, who were fighting under the umbrella of the United Nations (UN). The soldiers he was stationed with were charged with patrolling the swampy no-man's-land on the north side of the Imgin River — the new front line. The Canadian soldiers were supposed to venture into the no-man's-land, flush out the North Korean and Chinese soldiers, and then shoot them.

Lévesque found the guerrilla warfare in Korea even more disheartening than the type of strategic military strikes he had observed in Europe in World War II. "It was nothing more than an unimportant little war, but terribly dirty, sad, and depressing," he recalled.

Lévesque lived with the soldiers and shared all of their miseries: incessant rain, treacherous land mines, vicious spiders, and constant loneliness. In a famous *radio-verité* report, Lévesque recorded Québécois soldiers in the 22nd regiment who were taking refuge one night during a torrential rainstorm. The soldiers talked for hours about their nostalgia for home and their impressions of the Korean War. Lévesque recorded the soldiers' emotional outbursts without their knowledge — breaking a fundamental tenet of journalism — yet listeners back in Canada were touched by the candid stories.

Lévesque's star was rising at Radio-Canada. His reports on the Korean War were so impressive that the station considered overlooking his inferior radio voice. A couple of months after Lévesque's radio-verité scoop in Korea, Gérard Pelletier, a journalist at the highly respected newspaper *Le Devoir* wrote —

When he [Lévesque] speaks, we don't hear a Radio-Canada reporter. We hear a man from our milieu, a free man, who has brought our conscience, our hopes, our fears, and our curiosity with him. What he tells us, is exactly what we want to hear.

The brilliant young journalist was supposed to be in Korea for six months. However, two months into the assignment, Lévesque received an urgent telegram from Louise, who was having trouble coping with their two young children.

Shortly thereafter, Lévesque was recalled from Korea on compassionate grounds.

Following his trip to Korea, Lévesque returned to work with his colleagues at Radio-Canada's Montreal studios. While Lévesque respected and appreciated most of his colleagues, Judith Jasmin never failed to impress him. Lévesque admired her intellectual rigour, and Jasmin admired his talent for improvisation. Together, they worked long hours synthesizing outstanding radio reports. A feminist before the term was fashionable, Jasmin did not have any qualms about working with her male colleagues. The duo also worked well together on air — Lévesque's hoarse, raspy voice alternating with Jasmin's rich, melodious tones. It was inevitable that Lévesque, who had married out of a sense of obligation and who was frequently harangued by his wife about his workaholic tendencies, would find a soulmate in fellow journalist Jasmin.

The two professionals managed to keep their romantic inclinations at a simmering point until Radio-Canada sent them both to cover a mining story in northern Quebec in 1951. One day, when they sat down on a rock to rest momentarily, René leaned over and gently kissed Judith. She wrote in her diary, "It was as if I had known him and loved him in a former life!" René Lévesque and Judith Jasmin made a great couple. The only hitch was that Lévesque was married.

In 1952, Radio-Canada began to broadcast through the first French-language television station in Canada, CBFT.

Television screens flickered on in living rooms across the province, shattering Quebec's tradition of cultural isolation. By 1957, 80 percent of Quebeckers owned television sets. CBFT was an island of French culture in a sea of English popular culture, so it had to create all of its own programming. CBFT's Montreal studios soon became the largest French-language television production centre in the world.

Radio-Canada was not in a hurry to get Lévesque onto television. Although Lévesque was a gifted reporter with an eye for detail and an insatiable curiosity, his physical appearance was a bit of a deterrent for the brand-new communications medium. The unkempt, balding chain smoker was not an obvious choice for the television screen.

In the meantime, Lévesque continued his radio work. In the spring of 1953, Lévesque and Jasmin went to London to cover the coronation of Queen Elizabeth II. The reporters were stationed at the base of Nelson Column in Trafalgar Square for five hours, waiting for the royal coach to return to Buckingham Palace. They breathlessly invented fill-in about pigeons, church bells, and anything else they could think of. Then Jasmin and Lévesque came up with a story idea that had to be researched in France, so they would have a good excuse to "recover" in Paris for a few days.

Lévesque must have felt secure in his disdain for television on that day, because their live radio report was very exciting. Television footage, which had to be recorded in London and then flown to Canada for broadcasting, did not deliver the same punch as a live radio report. This discrepancy between the two media would not last long.

In the fall, Jasmin and Lévesque co-produced *Carrefour* (Crossroads) for Radio-Canada. This daily radio magazine brought Quebeckers a unique perspective on important national and international stories with interviews, documentaries, and investigative reports. Lévesque also left the studio occasionally to take the pulse of an issue via "streeters" (impromptu interviews with a random selection of pedestrians).

A year after their romantic escapade in Paris, René ended his affair with Judith Jasmin. She was devastated. Jasmin had hoped that Lévesque would eventually leave his wife for her. However, Lévesque was not prepared to abandon his family. He was not home often, but he wanted to have a home to return to at the end of the day.

Shortly after the death of Stalin, Lester Pearson, then the Canadian minister of external affairs, made a historic trip behind the Iron Curtain. He was to meet with a number of Soviet leaders and sell a little Canadian wheat and newsprint at the same time. Naturally, Radio-Canada's top journalist was there to report on the trip. Raised on a diet of anti-Soviet propaganda, Lévesque was amazed to discover that Russia was not just one big gulag. He expected to see a grim and desperate people. Instead, he saw Russian children in excellent health skipping through playgrounds, elderly people attending mass, and thousands of eager students walking around the capital with their noses in books. Stalin's sinister face still stared down from street corners, metro stations, and public squares across Moscow, yet Lévesque sensed that Russia was slowly beginning to open up to the outside world.

Pearson was in the midst of trade meetings with his Russian counterpart in Moscow when he was informed that there was someone who wanted to meet him on the Crimean peninsula. It was actually more of a summons than an invitation. The Canadian delegation flew south to Saki, where they were whisked away in ancient limousines for a short drive along a coastal road overlooking the Black Sea. They were on their way to Nikita Khrushchev's summer residence, a monstrous white villa with a stellar view.

Khrushchev, a jovial and stocky peasant with the bearing of a king, did not waste much time before launching into business. Shortly after their arrival, he asked Lévesque what the tape recorder was for. When Lévesque replied that it was for recording voices for radio, Khrushchev gestured that it should be turned on. Then he set upon Pearson like a vicious dog. Khrushchev was not interested in the mincing speech and the niceties of diplomacy. He provoked Pearson about the role of the North Atlantic Treaty Organization (NATO), insisting that it was an aggressive association, not a defensive one. Then he suggested that Canada should abandon NATO. Pearson was unprepared for such a blunt attack and he faltered in his responses to most of Khrushchev's comments. Every time Pearson tried to reply with a calm and logical comment, Khrushchev put him on the defensive. Later that night, the humiliated minister was coerced into drinking about 20 glasses of vodka and cognac with his Russian hosts.

On his way home, Lévesque saw headlines about the Pearson-Khrushchev duel in European newspapers. He had been obliged to share his information with reporters who could not make it to Khrushchev's residence. Naturally, when Lévesque learned that his report of this historic moment had never been broadcast on Radio-Canada, he was more than a little miffed. He discovered that his report had been sent to the Ministry of External Affairs for approval prior to broadcast. Lévesque was incensed, "The most colourful scoop of my career had been suppressed to protect the dignity of Lester Pearson."

In 1955, Radio-Canada brought *Carrefour* to television. And it gave Lévesque a real vote of confidence by providing him with a team of 10 people and an excellent broadcast slot, weeknights from 6:45 to 7:15 p.m. Due to technical limitations, most of the stories were about Montreal and its surrounding area, but there were a great variety of topics, from municipal affairs to medical stories. This current affairs show was very popular with viewers. By April 1956, 60 percent of televisions in Montreal homes were tuned in to *Carrefour*.

In 1956, the Lévesque household once again resonated with the sound of a crying baby. Suzanne, Lévesque's third child (and only girl) was born in February of that year. But there was trouble on the home front. Louise resented her husband's non-stop work schedule and his disinterest in parenting. Though she no longer complained very much, and was growing resigned to Lévesque's absence, her resentment was obvious.

In the fall of 1956, Lévesque reached the pinnacle of his broadcasting career with a new, live, half-hour newsmagazine called *Point de Mire*. The live show was scheduled for broadcast on Sunday nights at 11:15 p.m. The time slot made it clear that Radio-Canada did not expect this intellectual program to be popular with the general public. However, Lévesque knew that Quebeckers were more than ready to look beyond their provincial concerns. He wanted to be the man who would bring international news home to Quebeckers. Every week, *Point de Mire* focused on a different world event.

For its premiere on November 4, Lévesque turned his attention to Egyptian president Gamal Abdel Nasser's bold nationalization of the Suez Canal. This story was making headlines around the world, but Lévesque wanted to dig deeper in order to understand all of the relevant issues. Who constructed the canal? Why? What was Nasser's political background?

Each half-hour episode of *Point de Mire* took about 80 hours to piece together. The team began their work week with a hearty lunch on Wednesday. While juggling sandwiches and coffee, they flipped through the news publications, which were scattered across the table. Then the team bravely headed into a veritable storm of archival information, film clips, and news flashes.

Lévesque had the main responsibility; he had to explain all of the relevant issues of the story. So he spent hours upon hours cramming his brain with information at a downtown library. He tried to absorb about 10 times more information than he would actually have time to present, so he could improvise his monologue. Then on Sunday mornings, after having viewed the edited film sequence, Lévesque disappeared, with his cigarettes and a couple of headache tablets, to modify his text. Several hours later, he emerged in a blue cloud of smoke with a significantly reduced text. Finally, it was time for a rehearsal to make sure that Lévesque's monologue would fit it into the allocated time slot of 28 minutes, 25 seconds. His text was almost always too long, but when he was told to cut some of the text, Lévesque would invariably complain that there was nothing left to cut. Only one person, his producer Claude Sylvestre, had the patience to deal with Lévesque. When something went wrong, Sylvestre simply told Lévesque, "Okay René, you can swear for five minutes now, and then we'll discuss it." After another flurry of activity, Lévesque would appear on the set with a few minutes to spare.

A graphic depicting crosshairs would appear on the screen, accompanied by a few trumpet blasts. The announcer of *Point de Mire* introduced the show. Then the camera zoomed in on a small, balding man with a cigarette dangling from his lips. An announcer would say, "To guide you through this weekly labyrinth, here is René Lévesque ... "

Point de Mire was Lévesque's baby. He was completely in his element as he raced back and forth between an elementary-school-style blackboard and a giant world map, all the while scribbling significant dates and names in between cigarette puffs. Lévesque explored a range of socio-political issues, from unrest in Algeria to racism in America. As far as he was concerned, no issue was too complex to tackle, and he had a responsibility to help Quebeckers understand the world they lived in. His supreme tribute was when some *Point de Mire* fans protested because the Stanley Cup finals had driven the newsmagazine off the screen for a month.

Lévesque might have continued his meteoric rise in television had it had not been for a strike at Radio-Canada — which served as a launching pad for Lévesque's new profession — politician. In the fall of 1958, Radio-Canada producers wanted to negotiate several contractual issues, including job security and job descriptions. Their employer, the Canadian Broadcasting Corporation (CBC), informed the producers that they did not have the right to bargain for a collective agreement because they were considered management. Consequently, the producers formed a union affiliated with a confederation of Catholic trade unions and went on strike. The leader of this confederation was Jean Marchand, a former law school classmate of Lévesque's. Marchand had made a name for himself as a great orator, and was a highly respected union organizer as well.

At first, Lévesque was annoyed that his own producer,

Sylvestre, was going on strike, because Lévesque had been planning to go to Cuba to interview Fidel Castro. But after several weeks, he began to understand the producers' outrage at the CBC administration and at the English producers in Toronto who were not demonstrating solidarity. Lévesque threw himself into the strike with the same amount of fervour that he had devoted to *Point de Mire*. He helped create a stage show to raise money for the strike fund. "Temporary Difficulties" featured a variety of striking Radio-Canada employees presenting songs and skits. The star of the show was René Lévesque, with his clever *Point de Mire*-style reports on the strike situation. Over a period of almost three months, 20,000 spectators saw this show at the Comédie Canadienne theatre.

Lévesque and Marchand helped lead 1500 strikers to Parliament Hill in late January. When a small delegation arrived at the federal minister of labour's office, they were stunned to discover that Michael Starr was both unaware and unconcerned that the entire French-language service of Radio-Canada was on strike. Even after the Radio-Canada employees explained all of their grievances, Starr was disappointingly noncommittal.

When André Laurendeau, the editor of *Le Devoir*, heard Lévesque grumbling about the insensitivity of the federal government and the CBC administration to this Quebec crisis, he told Lévesque, "You know, listening to you, I have the impression you're headed straight for politics."

Chapter 4
The Nationalization Hero

One April evening in 1960, Jean Lesage, the handsome leader of the provincial Liberal party, was working on his election campaign at the Windsor Hotel in downtown Montreal. The campaign was already underway and Lesage had not yet finished creating his *équipe de tonnerre* (terrific team).

Lesage had offered Jean Marchand, the brilliant and fiery union organizer, a riding. However, Marchand had declined the invitation because he was preoccupied with union concerns. Now, Lesage was considering Marchand's friend, the outspoken television personality — René Lévesque.

As Lévesque walked towards the Windsor Hotel that night, he felt a bit disconcerted because his journalism career was at a standstill. Lévesque had completed the *Point de*

Mire season following the CBC producers' strike with a heavy heart. He knew that his show was going to be shelved.

One of the last *Point de Mire* stories had been about a loggers' strike in Newfoundland. Lévesque, a recent strike supporter himself, empathized with the loggers. Unfortunately, this sympathy was a little too obvious and, upon his return, Lévesque was criticized for his biased reporting. A Montreal columnist remarked that Lévesque's report appeared to be an editorial and not an objective investigation of the situation. It was becoming more and more obvious to Lévesque's friends and colleagues that he needed a bigger platform for his growing political consciousness. It was time to move out of the cramped television studio and onto the hustings.

It was after midnight when Lévesque arrived at the Windsor. Lesage was visibly fighting sleep as he opened the door to Lévesque. The two men greeted each other briefly, and then Lévesque announced that he was ready to enter the game of provincial politics. Lesage congratulated Lévesque on his decision and asked him to choose between two uncommitted ridings in the Montreal area, Laurier (northeast of downtown) and another one on the West Island. There was no contest. Lévesque immediately chose Laurier because he was familiar with this area after conducting countless hours of street interviews on the Plaza St-Hubert.

Lesage's campaign slogan "C'est le temps que ça change" (It's time for change) referred to his ardent desire to redevelop Quebec after years of patronage and pillaging by the Duplessis government.

As the leader and co-founder of the Union Nationale party, Maurice Duplessis had ruled Quebec with an iron fist almost continuously since 1936 (with a brief Liberal interlude during World War II). A former lawyer, Duplessis was a shrewd politician with a rock-solid power base formed by the Quebec business elite and the Catholic Church. Duplessis was not adverse to using blackmail and favouritism in order to stay in power. During his leadership, many public works projects, such as roads and hospitals, were constructed in appreciation for funds received from loyal constituencies.

Lévesque was drawn to Lesage's bold new plans for the future. He wanted to be part of the Liberal team that was planning to improve government accountability. Lévesque was impressed by Lesage's plans to rebuild the provincial police force from the ground up to eliminate entrenched corruption, as well as his plans to improve the provincial education system (Quebec had the lowest rate of school attendance in the country and 50 percent of Quebec children left school before the age of 15).

There was only one problem — a very cute and adorable problem. Lévesque had an illegitimate two-year-old daughter — the result of an affair with a Radio-Canada colleague. This baby threatened Lévesque's already shaky marriage, as well as his political career before it even began. Since most Quebeckers were devout Catholics, they were unlikely to disregard such impropriety. Although Lesage was not happy to hear about Lévesque's extramarital indiscretion, he agreed to support his new candidate, as long as Lévesque agreed to abandon his affair and try to repair his marriage. The identity of the toddler remained a well-kept secret.

Lévesque was a complete neophyte to politics, so Lesage put him under the care of Azellus Denis, the king of the neighbourhood and an experienced federal Liberal MP. Once, while Lévesque was on a provincial tour, he expressed concern that he was away from his riding too much. Lesage reassured him that Denis and his boys were looking after everything. Lévesque felt like an innocent lamb vis-à-vis the master politician ... "about as secure as one would feel if protected by a bunch of panthers purring while they sharpened their claws. For better or worse, however, my fate was in their paws."

One day when Denis and his protégé were out touring the Laurier neighbourhood, Lévesque met another local who would prove to be instrumental to his political career. Johnny Rougeau, a broad-shouldered, soft-hearted wrestling champion, decided to help out the new Liberal candidate with his extensive knowledge of the neighbourhood. Rougeau was tired of watching the Union Nationale steal elections, and he believed that Lévesque was an honest man who could bring about much-needed change. Denis and Rougeau introduced Lévesque to thousands of his potential electors, and he met most of them at home. The Liberal campaign organizers asked neighbours to gather in one house, so that Lévesque could meet with all of the people living on one street simultaneously. Not only were these meetings very efficient, they allowed Lévesque to speak to his potential electors in a comfortable and intimate setting. Ten years later, "kitchen meetings" would be a hallmark of Parti Québécois campaigning.

Campaigning was only part of the job. Lévesque and his organizers also spent an inordinate amount of time countering the Union Nationale's tactics to oust the Liberal candidate. The Union Nationale used every trick in the book in their efforts to defeat Lévesque, from circulating a photograph of Lévesque with Khrushchev (which played on electors' fear of Communism) to providing local priests with detailed information about Lévesque's extramarital affairs.

One of their dirtiest tricks was the invention of a phantom candidate to draw votes away from René Lévesque. At a time when only a small deposit was required in order to add a candidate to the ballot, it was easy for the Union Nationale to "invent" a new candidate. The phantom was an independent Liberal candidate and artist named René Lévesque. Incredibly, the ballot slip in the Laurier riding listed both René Lévesque the artist, and René Lévesque the journalist. Rougeau countered by driving around the neighbourhood with the vital message: "Vote for the real Lévesque — Lévesque the journalist!"

As the campaign wore on, the Laurier riding began to resemble the lawless wild west. The Union Nationale team resorted to even more aggressive tactics, including destroying a key Liberal organizer's car and torching a mailbox full of Liberal pamphlets.

On the day of the election, a gang of 100 big, strapping men organized by Rougeau prepared to defend the democratic process. Unfortunately, Union Nationale's thugs outnumbered Rougeau's improvised army, which was scattered throughout the neighbourhood. The thugs were able to slip into several polling stations and stuff ballot boxes with Union Nationale votes. Fortunately, at one poll, four honest women successfully fended off a gang of six Union Nationale mercenaries. The battle left one of the supervisors with an injury to her left arm.

Lévesque won Laurier by a hair. There were 14,012 votes for Lévesque and 13,833 for his Union Nationale opponent. (The phantom candidate won 910 votes!) In his acceptance speech following his victory, Lévesque thanked his electors and said, "The first thing we have to change is the kind of election rigging that we saw today. I even saw provincial police chaperoning bandits to the polling station."

The Liberal party won the election. Jean Lesage was at the helm of a new provincial government and a new political era.

René Lévesque, the brilliant and persuasive television personality, was obvious Cabinet material. After the election, Lesage invited his top candidates to join him at the Laurentian resort of St-Jovite. Lesage offered Lévesque the

Ministry of Social Welfare. However, Lévesque felt that he was destined for a grander portfolio, and he did not hesitate to tell Lesage his thoughts on the matter. He wanted an opportunity to have some impact on Quebec's destiny. By the end of the discussion, Lévesque had two ministries — Public Works and Hydraulic Resources.

Lesage's new government set to work with great enthusiasm. His *équipe de tonnerre* was going to shape a new and improved Quebec. For hundreds of years, French-Canadians had passively accepted economic colonization by English-Canadians and Americans. In 1960, French-Canadians represented 80 percent of the population of Quebec, yet they controlled only 10 percent of economic activity. Around the time that Lesage was elected, French-Canadians began to reject their status as cheap labour and recognized that the provincial government had the potential to reverse this economic inequality.

Lévesque, along with some other new Cabinet ministers, had no political experience. Lesage, on the other hand, had served as both parliamentary secretary and as minister of Resources and Development in the federal government. In the summer of 1960, while the sun shone and the playgrounds teemed with children, Lesage and his newly formed Cabinet hunkered down for a crash course in parliamentary protocol. Lesage's first goal was to eliminate the odious practice of political patronage that was destroying Quebec. He asked each minister to examine the files left by their Union

Nationale counterparts. And he ordered contracts that had been signed under the Duplessis regime to be annulled or renegotiated.

As Lévesque began to delve into his own filing cabinets, he discovered that the previous government had actually institutionalized corruption. Duplessis's treasurer had insisted that no contracts be awarded until the contractor had donated 10 percent of the bill to the party treasury. Many contractors were used to "buying" their contracts from the Public Works minister, and they were dumbfounded when they discovered that this was no longer the case.

Once the patronage clean-up was underway, Lesage outlined some of the areas that required reforms: education, health, police, and electoral practices. He also planned on creating three new government ministries to oversee federal-provincial affairs, cultural affairs, and natural resources. Lesage's modest goal was to update governmental structure and procedures in order to bring about a more transparent and democratic approach to public affairs. He got more than he bargained for. The feverish pace of change engendered by the Lesage administration set into motion a radical transformation of Quebec society, now known as "The Quiet Revolution." Lévesque's role in The Quiet Revolution was to mastermind the nationalization of Quebec's hydro-electric production.

When Lévesque took on the Hydraulic Resources portfolio, electricity was produced and distributed by almost a dozen separate companies, including Gatineau Power Co., Northern Quebec Power Co., and Shawinigan Water and Power. During Duplessis's reign, Quebec's natural resources were available to any private American or English-Canadian company that was interested in paying for the land concession. As a result, most of the profits from Quebec's natural resources were exported and Quebeckers did not benefit from their own resources. As well, the distribution of electricity in Quebec was disjointed because there was no cohesive distribution plan.

Hydro-Quebec, a state-run company created in 1944 by the Liberal Godbout government, was a major player in the energy production business. However, despite its significant size and wealth, most of Hydro-Quebec's power plant construction projects automatically went to a handful of American companies, including the Perini Company in Boston. In the Quebec "slush fund tradition" the Duplessis government routinely granted major contracts to companies that had contributed to the Union Nationale party.

Also, Lévesque knew that Quebec's demand for hydro-electric power was increasing exponentially. Hydro-Quebec would eventually be forced to go farther and farther afield in order to build new hydro-electric generator plants. Unfortunately, much of the land required for the creation of new installations and for the transmission of hydro-electric power belonged to private companies.

Lévesque and his team realized that the provincial

government needed to address all of these problems with a comprehensive policy. Hydro-electricity was Quebec's only native energy source. Quebeckers needed Hydro-Quebec to grow into an energy producer that was large enough to provide long-term economic security. However, private power utilities operated most of the hydro-electricity production in Quebec. It was becoming increasingly obvious to Lévesque and his team that the province needed to nationalize hydro-electricity.

This solution was not quite as obvious to the private power utilities or to Lévesque's Liberal colleagues. Even after discussing all the positive potential repercussions for Quebec consumers, there was general apprehension about using the word "nationalization."

Lévesque remembered an executive at one of the private utilities questioning whether Quebeckers could run the company as well as them. This type of remark brought back memories of the Suez Canal nationalization, which he had discussed on *Point de Mire*. Lévesque recalled that the British and French elite had shown the same paternalistic contempt when they had questioned the Egyptians' ability to operate the canal.

Lévesque surrounded himself with financial experts in order to draw up a nationalization strategy. One of his consultants was Jacques Parizeau, an economics professor at the prestigious École des Hautes Études Commerciales (University of Montreal's business school). Parizeau had been an occasional consultant on Lévesque's current affairs show *Point de Mire* in the 1950s. Parizeau along with a few other financial wizards calculated that the Lesage government would need to borrow $300 million in order to buy out the private power utilities. That amount was one-third of the Quebec government's annual budget. Lévesque knew that it was not going be easy to convince his colleagues to adopt this plan.

Parizeau and two colleagues went to New York City's financial district to research financing arrangements. (Montreal investment firms on St. James Street were too closely tied to the private utilities to consider loaning the Quebec government funds for the nationalization project.) After assuring Wall Street that they were not Communists, the Quebec delegation began to justify the necessity of the nationalization plan. One New York financier cut them short to tell them that what they were planning was nothing new — after all, Ontario had nationalized its hydro in 1907 — and that it would not be a problem to find the requisite $300 million.

Lévesque's team prepared a 130-page brief to convince the Liberal Cabinet that nationalizing hydro-electricity production would result in a more efficient and more cost-effective distribution network for Quebeckers. At the end of 1961, Lévesque travelled to northern Quebec to visit the construction site of Manic 5, Hydro-Quebec's future power plant. Lévesque was bowled over by the gigantic multiple-arch dam with its vast 800-square-mile reservoir. After touring the site, Lévesque joined some of the construction workers for a cup of coffee in Manic's vast cafeteria. The fact that Quebec engineers had conceived this incredible engineering project gave Lévesque renewed confidence in the nationalization plan.

Meanwhile, Lesage was handling backlash from unhappy private utilities, investment firms, and disgruntled Liberals. Lesage agreed in principle with Lévesque's nationalization plan. However, he believed that the process was moving much too fast, and he was genuinely concerned that Quebec could not finance such a grand plan.

Because this issue was causing a tremendous amount of tension among Liberal members of the legislature, in September 1962, Lesage convened the Cabinet and a few Liberal party officials to a secret caucus meeting in the Laurentian Mountains. The meeting was held at a government retreat, a modest log cabin near Lac-à-l'Epaule. On the first night, many of the ministers were in a foul mood because they believed the nationalization scheme was a big headache and a waste of everyone's time. The atmosphere was so poisonous that Lévesque considered going home. The next morning there was a debate between Lévesque and George Marler. Lévesque explained all of the financial and practical benefits of nationalization. Then Marler spoke eloquently about why the nationalization plan would be impossible to finance. Marler was Lesage's adviser and a minister without portfolio (he was also a holdover from a time when the Quebec premier needed an Anglophone by his side to deal with financial matters).

After lunch, Georges-Emile Lapalme, minister of Cultural

Affairs and the former head of the Liberal opposition, held forth on the controversial project. Lapalme supported the idea. He believed that it could happen. Then Lesage gave the project his own blessing. Lévesque did not know that Lesage had quietly been coming to the same conclusion as himself.

Lesage didn't just like the idea, he wanted to make it an election issue. He was so convinced of the feasibility and the urgent need for this project that he wanted to get the Quebec public's mandate. Soon Quebec was adorned with posters that reflected the province's new sense of pride and power. The nationalization of hydro-electricity was referred to as *la clé du royaume* (the key to the kingdom). Campaign imagery featured an image of a giant key decorated with a fleur-de-lis, the emblem of Quebec, and a clenched fist superimposed on a lightning bolt. Posters and pamphlets urged Quebeckers to support the new program: "Maintenant ou jamais! Maîtres chez nous" (Now or never! Masters of our own home). This powerful slogan, inspired by the nationalist vocabulary of the 1930s, promised Quebeckers a bright new future and deliverance from an English hegemony. Lévesque was buoyed by the success of his big gamble, although he sometimes worried that the highly charged campaign slogans were promising Quebeckers too much.

Lévesque toured the province, convincing Quebeckers of the virtues of nationalizing hydro-electricity. When some campaign organizers observed that Lévesque's speeches sometimes extended for three hours, they recommended that he make a *Point de Mire*-style film about the issue. Then Lévesque simply had to respond to audience questions, following the screening of the short film.

Lévesque was discouraged when a Québecois journalist asked whether Hydro-Quebec had enough experience to manage a province-wide network. The journalist's question typified Quebeckers' deeply entrenched inferiority complex. Since Quebeckers had been running Hydro-Quebec competently for 18 years, why doubt that Hydro-Quebec could manage a province-wide network?

On election day, November 14, 1962, Quebeckers demonstrated their confidence in Lesage's government and in the nationalization plan. The Liberals swept back into office with 12 more seats than they had won in 1960. The Quebec government obtained $300,000 from more than 40 U.S. financial institutions, and then it began to buy out the disparate private hydro-electric utilities across the province.

After the nationalization of hydro-electric production, Quebeckers gained a new sense of pride, and the price of hydro power decreased for thousands of Quebec households. By 1965, Quebeckers had the least expensive electricity in North America.

Douglas Fullerton, a prominent economist who had helped launch this project, later said, "The nationalization of electricity was one of the most rational and best executed financial transactions I have had the privilege to see in my whole career."

Chapter 5
Birth of a Separatist

Lévesque was extremely proud of the nationalization of hydro-electricity in Quebec, and the success of this bold venture prompted him to imagine other projects that would enable Quebeckers to exert more control over their destiny. In the meantime, Lévesque was a minister in Lesage's government.

Several pivotal issues in the mid-1960s forced Lévesque to confront his growing separatist yearnings. One of them was the Fulton-Favreau formula, a legal mechanism to amend the constitution once it was repatriated (removed from British jurisdiction and placed under Canadian jurisdiction). In 1965, Lesage proposed a resolution to ratify Fulton-Favreau. Fulton-Favreau ensured that there could be no fundamental changes to the constitution without the agreement of all provincial governments as well as the federal government. Also, Quebec was given a special right to veto any change that was not in its favour.

Jean Lesage was satisfied with the proposed reform and he moved heaven and earth to try and have the Fulton-Favreau formula accepted by the provincial legislature. However, he did not succeed because nationalist Quebeckers believed that greater powers should be accorded to Quebec before any discussion of patriation. The nationalists also worried the veto could ultimately be used to penalize Quebeckers. They believed that if Quebec used its veto to prevent the adoption of a national program, then other provinces might retaliate and prevent Quebec from achieving its goals.

Lesage requested that Lévesque publicly defend the Fulton-Favreau formula in a debate with Jacques-Yvan Morin, a professor of constitutional law at the University of Montreal. When Lévesque tried to convince the students that Fulton-Favreau would protect Quebec from a federal offensive, the strident nationalist students openly booed him. Lévesque felt deeply humiliated. After the debate, Claude Ryan, the editor of *Le Devoir* newspaper, told Lévesque, "I think that you would be wise to pay more attention to constitutional questions. They could become more important than you think this evening."

Lévesque was increasingly frustrated, but he had not yet figured what to do about it. When the Laurier riding secretary boldly suggested that Lévesque should found a nationalist party, Lévesque was shocked. Over the next two years, Lévesque's political aspirations continued to diverge from the Liberal party agenda.

Meanwhile, Lévesque had a new portfolio to manage. After Émilien Lafrance left the Cabinet, Lesage handed Lévesque a new challenge — the Ministry of Family and Social Welfare. In the mid-1960s, social services were still under the control of the Catholic Church to a large degree. Duplessis had been content to let the church worry about the desperate members of society: single mothers, the elderly, invalids, and the handicapped. When the new minister began to tour the province's orphanages and hospices, he was horrified by the level of misery he found there, and astonished by popular attitudes towards disadvantaged Quebeckers. Many people honestly believed that terrible suffering should be accepted as part of the divine will of God.

Thousands of Quebeckers were in dire straits: 38 percent of Montreal families were living in poverty, 53,000 single mothers were caring for their children on an annual budget of less than $2000 per year, and Quebec was teeming with unwanted babies. Fueled by a desire to replace the concept of charity with an investment in social services, Lévesque began to overhaul the social assistance program at breakneck speed. "Instead of subsidizing poverty, we're going to sustain the essential needs of the family," he promised.

One of Lévesque's bright new social services policies

brought him into conflict with Ottawa. During World War II, the federal government had set up a family allowance plan to assist large families. Lévesque thought it made more sense for family allowance to be administered at the provincial level. In 1966, after he devised a disbursement system that would be more beneficial to large families, Lévesque shared his recommendations at a federal-provincial conference of welfare ministers. Prime Minister Lester B. Pearson wasn't interested. Lévesque left the meeting, frustrated by Ottawa's paternalistic attitude towards Quebec. Lévesque was dissatisfied with the status quo. He felt that the federal government did not recognize Quebec's special status and that Quebec needed to have more control over its social and economic destiny. It would be several years before Lévesque put his thoughts into action.

Around Easter of 1966, Lévesque was on a rare holiday with Louise and their three children. They had just arrived in Bermuda to enjoy the crystalline blue water, the warm sand, and the much-needed break from day-to-day routine. It was not meant to be. The family had barely settled into their hotel when Lévesque received an urgent call from a Lesage aide. Soon he was off to join the premier at his winter golfing base in Miami. Lesage was gearing up for another election, and he wanted to discuss strategy.

The Liberals knew that Daniel Johnson's Union Nationale party and a few upstart nationalist parties would likely attract a number of voters, but they still felt pretty confident.

While reviewing a public opinion survey of voting patterns, Lesage and his supporters made the mistake of assuming that the "undecided" and "unwilling to participate" voters (who made up almost 40 percent of the population) would decide to cast their ballots in proportion to the prevailing tendencies.

Back in Quebec, Lévesque began to have doubts about the new campaign. Compared to the riveting campaigns of 1960 and 1962, this latest flurry of public relations activity appeared to be slapdash and lacking a clear and powerful platform. Lesage's autocratic approach did not help. Despite a brilliant collection of Cabinet ministers who masterminded key reforms during the Quiet Revolution — Lesage was portrayed as the star, alone in most of the campaign imagery. Posters depicted Lesage chatting with mothers and children, Lesage in his shirt-sleeves at a factory, and Lesage in a felt hat talking to a farmer.

Lévesque and Gérin-Lajoie, two of Lesage's most illustrious ministers, were not even invited to the official opening of the campaign in Sherbrooke, a town in the Eastern Townships. However, Lévesque decided to go anyway. When the crowd caught a glimpse of him, they rose in a standing ovation. Lesage was visibly upset and asked his organizers to take Lévesque aside, so he couldn't steal the show. Lesage was becoming increasingly irritable and aggressive. Some Liberal ministers worried that Lesage would be the author of his own defeat.

The Union Nationale party benefited from the public's waning interest in Lesage, as did a few burgeoning nationalist parties, such as the Rassemblement Pour l'Independence (RIN), the Regroupement National, and the Ralliement National. The RIN — the most popular of the new nationalist parties — advocated the separation of Quebec from the rest of Canada. RIN leader Pierre Bourgault's angry, radical speeches scared Lévesque. He knew that extreme nationalism was a dangerous force that could transform "civilized" people into barbarians. Lévesque recalled the Dachau concentration camp as a sobering example of nationalism gone wrong.

In 1963, the newly formed Front Libération Québec (FLQ) had begun a terrorism campaign against symbols of the English elite — toppling the Wolfe monument on the Plains of Abraham — and bombing mailboxes in a wealthy, predominantly English-speaking Montreal neighbourhood. There were wellsprings of nationalism across Quebec, and Lévesque worried that many Quebeckers were not prepared to be patient.

In June 1966, the Union Nationale came back into power, with Daniel Johnson at the head. Johnson's slogan, "Égalité ou Independence" (Equality or Independence), was a chef d'oeuvre of ambiguity. It persuaded federalists that he was simply defending Quebec autonomy, while convincing nationalists that Quebec would gain more power.

The Liberals formed a reasonable opposition force with about 47 percent of the popular vote, but the real surprise was that almost 9 percent of the vote had gone to the nationalist parties. Lévesque won his Laurier seat again, so he returned to Quebec City in the Liberal opposition.

Lévesque's ego suffered from the sudden loss of power and prestige. One day he was a Cabinet minister; the next day, he was a regular member of the legislature for the Laurier riding. Lévesque had never really enjoyed parliamentary debate because it felt like a never-ending partisan game. Now, participation in these debates was one of his key roles. Lévesque was also disappointed because after only eight months as the minister of Family and Social Welfare, he had barely begun to execute some of his grand ideas for social assistance reform.

When Lévesque was invited to write a column for the weekly paper, *Dimanche-matin*, he jumped at the opportunity to return to journalism. Lévesque was enthused by the opportunity to write about his opinions on a wide range of current issues, from health insurance to the bias of private radio stations. His friends and colleagues observed that he was much more focused on his weekly column than his political obligations.

Eric Kierans had been a good friend of Lévesque for years. Both men had served as ministers in Lesage's government, and they respected one another. Both were individualists and rebels who liked to stir things up. On the tennis court, they worked together seamlessly as a doubles pair — Lévesque smashed balls near the net, while Kierans took care of the long shots from the back of the court. Yet Lévesque and Kierans lived in very different worlds. Kierans was an English millionaire from Hampstead, who had served as president of the Montreal Stock Exchange prior to joining the Lesage government. Lévesque was a plain-spoken man from the Gaspé hinterland, who had never been motivated by money. After the Liberal defeat in 1966, internal party conflict forever destroyed Lévesque and Kieran's friendship.

In the summer of 1966, Lévesque called a few friends together to consider Quebec's political future. Eric Kierans, Paul Gérin-Lajoie, new Members of the National Assembly François Aquin and Yves Michaud, and a few other disgruntled Liberals met with Lévesque in a country home near Lake Memphramagog in the Eastern Townships. They wanted to discuss organizational changes to the Liberal party. While, conservative Liberals close to Lesage were convinced the Liberals had lost the election because of their overly ambitious agenda, the reformist group viewed the Quiet Revolution as a mere warm-up exercise, with the best yet to come.

As summer became fall, the reform committee grew into a group of about 100 Liberals who met on a regular basis at the now-defunct St. Denis Club on Sherbrooke Street in Montreal. The members were all interested in change, however, they were not all interested in pursuing separatism. At the Liberal convention in November 1966, Eric Kierans stated, "I don't think that the time is ripe for Quebec to go it alone, without suffering a serious drop in its standard of living."

Lévesque's opinions were growing more discordant

within the reform committee, although he did not yet openly support a nationalist platform. Many conservative Liberals began to identify Lévesque as a key troublemaker. Some suggested that Lévesque's resignation would resolve most of the Liberal party's troubles.

On April 1 and 2, 1967, 20 Liberals held a private meeting at a hotel in Mont-Tremblant, a resort town in the Laurentians about two hours north of Montreal. Paul Gérin-Lajoie and Robert Bourassa (a brilliant economist and Lesage's trusted adviser) opened the discussion with a proposal to reform federalism so that Quebec could have special status within Canada. As Lévesque listened to their arguments, he scribbled incessantly.

When Lévesque was asked for his opinion, he dropped a bombshell. Lévesque described the concept of sovereignty-association for the first time. For 30 minutes, Lévesque held forth on his now well-defined view of Quebec as a sovereign nation that would negotiate economic associations with the rest of Canada. The meeting had started on April Fool's Day, but Lévesque was dead serious as he described the broad strokes of the future Parti Québécois's agenda. Most of the attendees were in shock. They knew that Lévesque's radical plan would never be accepted by the Liberal party.

A few months later, the president of France, General Charles de Gaulle, dropped his own bombshell. That summer, Montreal hosted Expo '67, an international exhibition to celebrate Canada's centennial anniversary. The city was bursting with pride. De Gaulle arrived in Montreal to visit Expo on a blistering hot day at the end of July. An ebullient crowd gathered in the Place Jacques Cartier, a picturesque square across the street from Montreal's City Hall. When de Gaulle mentioned that he wanted to speak to the crowd, an obliging Radio-Canada employee offered to hook up the microphone on the City Hall balcony.

After the French president acknowledged the crowd below, he exclaimed, "Vive Montréal! Vive le Québec!" (Long live Montreal! Long live Quebec!). Then he bellowed, "Vive le Quebec libre!" (Long live a free Quebec!) The crowd below was incredulous. Did he really say that? What did he mean? No one will ever know how spontaneous de Gaulle's comments were. But what is known is that those four words had a great deal of impact. Some Quebeckers were so excited they danced in the streets. The prime minister, Pierre Elliott Trudeau, was absolutely furious.

Lévesque was stunned by de Gaulle's incendiary comment. However, he was not interested in praising the president like some young radical Quebeckers who chanted, "Quebec libre, oui, oui, oui. Quebec libre, de Gaulle l'a dit" (Free Quebec yes, yes, yes. Free Quebec, that's what de Gaulle said). If Quebec was going to take control of its own destiny, then Lévesque wanted it to be a home-grown idea. After centuries of domination by an English-speaking elite, it would be unconscionable to let a foreign president dictate Quebec's future.

After the historic Mont Tremblant meeting, federalist

Liberals began to withdraw from the reform committee. Paul Gérin-Lajoie left the group to write up his own proposal. Now Lévesque and his faithful followers were so few in number that they could meet in the basement of Bourassa's home in the Town of Mount Royal, a prosperous Montreal suburb.

In August, Lévesque went on his annual pilgrimage to the sea. Ever since 1955, when Lévesque and his young family had first visited Cape Cod, Lévesque had vacationed on the beaches of the American east coast. Lévesque appreciated the temperature of the ocean water (warmer than the Gaspé) and his anonymity in the American coastal resorts. Lévesque had been fascinated by the United States for most of his life, and he enjoyed spending time there. The little boy who grew up in pre-World War II Quebec — a conservative and isolated society — was greatly impressed by the Americans' verve and initiative. A self-described "Yankébécois" (Yankee Québécois), Lévesque felt more at home in the United States than he did in English-speaking Canada. He once said, "As much as Canada outside Quebec seemed to me, generally, to be a sad collective grey, the United States never ceased to fascinate me."

Upon Lévesque's return from the United States, he presented the reform committee with a manifesto for achieving the state of sovereignty-association. Lévesque intentionally avoided using the term independence because the radical RIN had appropriated this term, and now "independence" had violent overtones. At the age of 45, Lévesque was ready to dedicate the rest of his life to the promotion of Quebec sovereignty.

In mid-September, Lévesque summed up the key arguments of sovereignty-association in a 35-page document entitled *Option-Québec*. The manifesto featured a famous Franklin D. Roosevelt quote: "The only thing we have to fear is fear itself." United States President Roosevelt had first uttered this phrase during the economic depression of the 1930s. It was meant to help the American public overcome their desperate fear of unemployment and poverty. Lévesque decided to use this quote in 1967 because he was trying to inspire Quebeckers to believe in their own potential to control their cultural and economic destiny.

Option-Québec, Lévesque's rallying cry to the Quebec public, was a series of logical arguments that justified the pursuit of sovereignty-association — Quebeckers have a unique language and culture; the Quiet Revolution proved that they are capable of achieving grand schemes; the federal government is a roadblock that prevents Quebeckers from fulfilling their potential — therefore, sovereignty-association is the only solution.

Lévesque was eager to announce his bold plan at the upcoming Liberal convention. However, by the time of the convention in mid-October 1967, it was painfully obvious that Lévesque had strayed so far from the Liberal Party's position that he was now persona non grata. Lévesque was on his way out. What would happen first — would he volunteer to leave the Liberal party or would he be forced out?

On Friday, October 13, the provincial Liberal party

convened at the majestic Château Frontenac Hotel, which sits on a cliff overlooking the St. Lawrence River. Hostesses dressed in chic, red cocktail dresses greeted the convention delegates. Lévesque sensed the level of fear in the room as soon as he heard the convention regulations — voting would occur by raised hand instead of a secret ballot — and no amendments to constitutional resolutions would be tolerated. He knew that party members were unlikely to vote in favour of a controversial issue by raised hand.

Premier Jean Lesage arrived with Eric Kierans. When Lesage spoke about all of the negative repercussions of sovereignty-association, Lévesque wondered whether he should even bother to state his position the next day. He left the convention hall before Lesage finished his speech.

On the second day of the convention, Gérin-Lajoie eloquently introduced his proposal to review Canadian federalism and to promote Quebec's special status. When Lévesque was given a chance to respond, he leapt to his feet with a few notes in hand and used an architectural analogy to discuss political arrangements in Canada. He explained that if Confederation is a split-level house, then endorsing Gérin-Lajoie's proposal would be like adding a semi-detached floor to one level of the house. Wouldn't it be easier to start from scratch with the construction materials and build two new semi-detached houses?

Following a heated four-hour debate, Lévesque announced that he was going to leave the Liberal party and that he would take his ideas with him. Very few people acknowledged Lévesque as he left the hotel ballroom. Most convention attendees sat very still, staring vacantly at the ceiling, relieved that the troublemaker was finally leaving.

It was not a traumatic break-up for Lévesque. He had helped the Liberal party achieve monumental reforms, and the Liberal party had helped Lévesque gain some political experience. Now the relationship was over, due to irreconcilable differences.

That night, Lévesque and a group of his supporters had dinner at The Old Homestead Restaurant in Quebec City. At the end of the meal, one of the supporters suggested that everyone who was present sign their names on one placemat, because he had a sense that it was a historic night.

Chapter 6
Growing Pains

Lévesque barely had a chance to collect his thoughts after leaving the morose Liberal convention, before he found himself surrounded by hundreds of enthusiastic young people. "When he left [the Liberal party] he took with him not only a fair number of youthful supporters but most of the party's crusading spirit, too," wrote the *Montreal Gazette*'s political correspondent. The Mouvement Soveraineté-Association (MSA) was born of disenchanted Liberals who wanted to pursue their nationalist goals within a new political party, and young Quebeckers who pinned all their hopes and dreams for an independent Quebec on Lévesque. The MSA was not the first separatist movement in the history of Quebec. In fact, there had been a regular ebb and flow of separatist passions ever since 1837, when Louis-Joseph Papineau and *les Patriotes* led an armed rebellion against their British rulers.

The French-Canadian people had evolved as a unique society following the defeat of their French colonial rulers on the Plains of Abraham in 1759. They did not identify with France, the land of their forefathers. Yet, they did not identify with English-Canadians either, due to linguistic and cultural differences. The romantic ideal of nationhood beckoned.

Now that Lévesque was free to pursue his vision untrammelled by the constraints of the Liberal party, he began to traverse the province, promoting his new vision of sovereignty-association. In January 1968, *Option-Québec*, Lévesque's political manifesto with statements of support from Parizeau and other prominent Quebeckers, was launched at the Prince-Charles restaurant in Montreal. Intellectuals, students, and journalists crowded into the restaurant and jostled to see the new nationalist leader and to hear him articulate his plan to achieve sovereignty-association. Approximately 50,000 copies of the booklet were sold in record time. The MSA grew quickly, from 700 sympathizers in January 1968 to 7000 a few months later.

In the spring of 1968, snowbanks were melting, purple and white crocuses were poking through the ground, and Lévesque had a new bounce in his step. Not only was he exhilarated by the groundswell of support for sovereignty-association, he also had a new love in his life.

In March, Lévesque had met Corinne Côté at a Quebec

City press conference to promote *Option-Québec*. Following their introduction by a mutual friend, both Lévesque and Côté experienced a *coup de foudre*. The svelte 24-year-old student with fine Native features and a penchant for mini-skirts was drawn to the 45-year-old politician with a reputation as an *agent provocateur*, and the feeling was mutual. Later that evening, when Corinne joined Lévesque and his companions for dinner at a local hangout for journalists and politicians, she discovered that Lévesque had saved a place next to him. He was anxiously awaiting her arrival.

Lévesque had a great talent for seducing women. Corinne later said, "He was always a bit awkward physically … he would have liked to have been a bit taller, to have had a bit more hair. So I think that is why he liked to seduce women — so he could convince himself that he could be seductive." When Corinne began to receive love letters from her new lover, she was touched by his romantic sensibilities.

Corinne was also fascinated by Lévesque's proposal for sovereignty-association. Her father had worked for Price Paper in Alma (near Chicoutimi) for 38 years, at a time when it was necessary to speak English to advance to the foreman level. As their relationship developed, Lévesque took on the role of mentor. Corinne wanted to learn more about politics, literature, and world history, and Lévesque was more than happy to teach her.

In mid-April, almost 2000 people gathered for the first sovereigntist convention at the Maurice Richard Arena in east end Montreal. The boisterous crowd of students, intellectuals, and young professionals were almost all Montrealers and half of them were under 30 years of age. Clearly, the MSA would need to attract a more diverse support base, including rural inhabitants and the working class, in order to become a serious contender on the political scene.

For the most part, the delegates agreed with Lévesque's bold vision of a negotiated and peaceful transition from the province of Quebec to a sovereign nation in which French is the official language. And who could argue with other idealistic MSA objectives, such as implementing a higher minimum wage, equal pay for women, or compulsory civic service for young people?

However, when the delegates began to discuss English-language rights, the debate became so heated that it threatened to divide the new political movement. François Aquin, one of the most enthusiastic former members of the Liberal reform group, was renowned for his hard-line position. Convinced that the "historical rights" of Anglophones were merely privileges, Aquin suggested that English schools should be denied government subsidies. When the convention crowd applauded Aquin's proposal, it sent a chill down Lévesque's spine. It seemed like some of the RIN's radical, intolerant philosophy was beginning to seep into the MSA. Not only would abolishing public English schools smack of bigotry, but it would almost certainly result in a barrage of negative international press. Ultimately, Lévesque knew that the MSA's treatment of Quebec's English-speaking minority would be a testament to the party's maturity.

The issue of language was becoming increasingly complex, due to immigration. Many MSA members were concerned that the French language was in jeopardy because the falling birth rate of Quebeckers was compounded by immigrant Anglicization. In the 1960s, most immigrants to Quebec either spoke English when they arrived or chose to learn English as their second language. Some nationalists believed that without a political response to this situation Francophones would eventually become a minority population in Quebec.

In 1968, this situation came to a head in Saint-Léonard, a suburb in northeast Montreal. Before World War II, Saint-Léonard was primarily a French-speaking working class community. During the 1950s and 1960s, Italian immigrants began to move into this neighbourhood, and by 1966, almost 30 percent of the population was of Italian origin. The children grew up speaking Italian and English. In 1968, the Italian population requested English schools for their children.

A protest movement, called the Movement pour l'intégration scolaire (MIS), was created in response to this demand for increased Anglicization. The MIS believed that Saint-Léonard's Italian families should be forced to send their children to French schools, and they mounted an aggressive campaign to promote their message. The schoolyard of Aimé-Renaud became a focal point for demonstrations;

the RIN that summer because he did not want the MSA to be contaminated by the violent radicalism of the RIN. Besides which, many of the more moderate RIN members had already joined the MSA. Then Lévesque pursued Gilles Grégoire, leader of the Ralliement National (RN), a relatively conservative nationalist party, based in the rural regions of Lac-Saint-Jean, Northwestern Quebec, and the Gaspé. After absorbing about 5000 Ralliement National (RN) members, the MSA had an astounding 20,000 members across the province. The MSA was building momentum, and it was ready to evolve into a political party.

In October 1968, the members of the MSA gathered in Quebec City for a historic convention that gave birth to the new Parti Québécois (PQ). Lévesque would have preferred a party name that included the word "sovereignty," but Grégoire convinced him that that sounded too intellectual for most rural Quebeckers. The delegates gathered to establish official party policies and statutes based on the draft that had been drawn up at the April MSA convention. Then they debated resolutions from regional groups. During the calm methodical discussion about how the PQ would achieve sovereignty-association, Lévesque laid out some ground rules for the new political party. For instance, Lévesque was adamant that financing of the PQ should be transparent and that there should not be any strings attached to donations.

The PQ was the first political party to make nationalism a respectable issue, due to Lévesque's rejection of extreme and violent manifestations of nationalism. As a result, many Quebeckers began to trust that the PQ's pursuit of sovereignty-association would be a peaceful and negotiated process.

After watching the PQ convention on television, Pierre Bourgault realized that the Parti Québécois represented serious political competition to the RIN. Bourgault decided to dissolve his own party to prevent the nationalist vote from being divided too many ways. Lévesque was not entirely pleased when he heard about the RIN's suicide. First, the existence of the extreme left-wing RIN had helped the MSA to be viewed as the "safer" moderate option. Second, Lévesque was concerned that now that Bourgault was without a party, he would try to get into the PQ executive.

About a year later, Jacques Parizeau joined the party, and the PQ gained more respectability and credibility in the financial domain. Parizeau believed in the feasibility of Quebec independence, and he wasn't worried about its potential financial impact on Quebeckers. As far as he was concerned, "Capitalists invest in more than 75 countries, and they have already adapted to almost every kind of political system. It's uncertainty that makes them afraid, not independence."

The PQ continued to grow rapidly and to gain ground among middle-class people. This situation alarmed Pierre Trudeau, who had once dismissed the PQ as a mere "particle." Despite the fact that the PQ was a legitimate political party and not a terrorist organization, Trudeau requested that the RCMP spy on the PQ and "provide a detailed report on the present state of separatism in Quebec, in terms of organization, numbers involved, strategy, and outside influence."

A provincial election was called for April. The Quebec public was concerned about unemployment, so Bourassa (the new Liberal leader) focused his campaign on getting Quebeckers back to work: "Québec au travail." Bourassa also used a sensational media campaign to warn the electorate about the PQ's separatist agenda. For instance, one image featured a man sawing through the very branch that he was sitting on. The implied message was that separation would result in lower salaries, the loss of federal benefits, and a reduced quality of life for Quebeckers.

Meanwhile, Lévesque was trying to tone down the sentimental pull for independence and he was promoting the social and economic benefits of sovereignty-association. He also wanted Quebeckers to be inspired by the example of small, sovereign countries around the world. He pointed out that Sweden and Switzerland, similar in land and population size to Quebec, were very successful economically, socially, and politically.

Two days before the election, the "Brinks affair" added fuel to the fire of separatist fear. A convoy of nine Brinks armoured trucks loaded with millions of dollars worth of securities left the head office of Royal Trust in Montreal at dawn and travelled down Highway 401 to Toronto. Montreal's English newspapers sensationalized this event, causing the Quebec public to worry that the threat of separation was triggering a flight of capital. The *Montreal Gazette* claimed to have a photo of the convoy that it would not publish for fear of setting off general panic.

On April 29, Bourassa and the Liberal party swept into power as expected. However, the PQ was amazed to learn that it had won 23 percent of the popular vote. Pundits estimated that half of all French-speaking Montrealers had voted for the PQ.

Seven PQ candidates won their ridings, including Claude Charron, a 23-year-old candidate who won Saint-Jacques; Camille Laurin, a psychiatrist who won Bourget; and Robert Burns, a dedicated labour lawyer who won Maisonneuve. Lévesque did not win his Laurier seat. Although the electorate appreciated Lévesque, they were wary of his new politics. Laurier's considerable immigrant population was pleased to be part of Canada, and they didn't want that relationship to change.

A huge crowd of PQ supporters were waiting for Lévesque when he entered Paul Sauvé Arena. He had lost his own seat, and his party had not won as many seats as anticipated. Lévesque sensed that the crowd was tense with nervous energy. "Don't you find that this defeat has the smell of victory?" asked Lévesque, and the arena erupted with applause. This was no time to cry — the PQ was just getting off the ground.

Lévesque was absolutely drained. He had been burning the candle at both ends during the campaign leading up to the April election, and now he was unemployed. Instead of appreciating his forced break, Lévesque's initial reaction was to sulk and ponder resigning from the PQ leadership.

At that point, Lévesque decided to invite Corinne Côté to live with him. Lévesque was besotted with Corinne, and he had gained a new serenity since their relationship began. Whenever Lévesque dropped into an emotional tailspin, Corinne knew the right words to calm him. Considering that his marriage was a charade (Lévesque was little more than a visitor at the Woodbury Avenue home where his estranged wife lived with their children) and that he had found true love with Corinne, moving out permanently was inevitable.

The couple found an apartment downtown at 1400 Pine Avenue. Corinne chose it (her brother also lived in the building) so she wouldn't be lonely when Lévesque went off on political errands. Lévesque refused to take a salary from the PQ, so the couple lived frugally at the Pine Avenue apartment. Their living conditions were those of university students — some of their furniture was composed of wooden crates.

The summer of *la dolce vita* was spent playing tennis at a friend's cottage in the Laurentians, fixing up the new apartment, and writing a column for the tabloid newspaper *Le Journal de Montréal*. In the years to come, Lévesque would find this column very useful for having his voice heard among Quebeckers.

Chapter 7
The Parti Québécois: A Serious Political Contender

The Parti Québécois was a responsible, democratic political party that denounced the use of violence to achieve political ends. However, in the early 1960s, some extreme nationalist groups were so impatient for independence that they did resort to violence. The Front de Libération du Québec (FLQ), formed in 1963, began bombing armouries and mailboxes in Montreal.

Then the FLQ upped the ante. On October 5, 1970, members of the FLQ kidnapped James Cross, a British trade commissioner, from his Westmount home in Montreal. The hostage-takers said they would release Cross in exchange for: the release of 17 FLQ political prisoners, a "voluntary" contribution of $500,000, a flight to Algeria or Cuba, and the broadcast of their political manifesto.

Trudeau made it very clear to Bourassa, the new premier of Quebec, that they must not give in to blackmail from a terrorist organization. And there was no question of releasing the imprisoned FLQ members. After all, these men were not "political" prisoners, they were common criminals who had committed serious offences, such as armed robbery.

Ottawa agreed to only one of the FLQ's requests — to broadcast their political manifesto — because the text was deemed to be so coarse and simplistic that it would probably backfire on the FLQ. A couple of days later, Jérôme Choquette, the provincial minister of Justice, went on television to inform Quebeckers that the provincial government was employing a tough uncompromising position vis-à-vis the hostage-takers. He explained that if a society gives in to blackmail, then social order is in jeopardy.

Barely 30 minutes after Choquette's statement, the FLQ took their second victim. On October 10, a beautiful warm Saturday evening, Pierre Laporte (the provincial minister of Labour and Immigration) was playing ball with his nephew outside his home in Saint-Lambert, a suburb on Montreal's south shore, when he was kidnapped. News of this second kidnapping sent shock waves throughout Quebec.

Bourassa, who must have imagined that he could be the next victim, retreated to the 20th floor of the Queen Elizabeth Hotel with his Cabinet. Police armed with machine guns patrolled the floor while the shell-shocked premier and his ministers attempted to find a solution to the crisis. On the night of Laporte's kidnapping, Bourassa had contacted Trudeau about sending in the army and dusting off the War Measures Act. Bourassa was in a tailspin of panic. He did not believe that Quebec could handle the crisis on its own.

Lévesque was increasingly concerned about the Bourassa government's intransigent position vis-à-vis the hostage-takers. He genuinely believed the hostages' lives might be spared if the provincial government was prepared to negotiate with the FLQ. A host of other small "l" liberal Quebeckers were also concerned about the way that the crisis was being handled. Lévesque wrote a statement requesting that the provincial government resolve the problem on its own and that they exercise a bit more moderation. Then Lévesque, Claude Ryan, and 14 other influential Quebeckers, including union leaders, politicians, and academics, signed the document.

Meanwhile, Bourassa rushed headlong toward an even more extreme position. On October 16, letters from Bourassa and from Jean Drapeau, the mayor of Montreal, requesting the presence of the Canadian army in Montreal as well as the proclamation of the War Measures Act (WMA), were delivered to Trudeau's office in the middle of the night. One hour later, the federal Cabinet approved both of these requests.

The WMA is legislation of last resort. It is designed to restore public order in the event of a war, invasion, or insurrection, either real or perceived. The WMA gives police the right to enter and search any premises without a warrant, as well as the right to arrest anyone that they deem to be suspicious. The accused can be kept in custody without the right to consult a lawyer. The WMA was modelled on a British law that was adopted at the beginning of World War I. The British law was dropped at the end of the war.

In the early hours of October 16, the military occupation of Montreal began. A convoy of military vehicles transported thousands of soldiers downtown. Then three giant Hercules planes arrived at Saint-Hubert airport with hundreds more soldiers to guard city hall and other government buildings. Montrealers awoke to an occupied city. And the police began to act on the WMA proclamation. They scoured the city of Montreal in a desperate attempt to find Laporte and Cross, as well as any FLQ cells. Four hundred Quebeckers, including artists and journalists who dared to question established authority, were arrested and placed in custody.

At the height of the crisis, 87 percent of Quebeckers supported the use of the WMA because they were terrified. However, Lévesque was not convinced that the WMA and the military occupation of Montreal were really necessary, and he was deeply disturbed by the use of drastic measures that denied basic civil rights. Lévesque's October 17 column in *Le Journal de Montréal* reflected his despair —

Quebec no longer has a government. The stump of a one we did have was swept away at the first really hard blow. Bourassa's cabinet has turned in its hand and is no longer anything but a puppet of the federal rulers. It is now clear from the very beginning of this tragic period marked by the kidnapping of Mr. Cross, this government has only had a bit player's role ... that [federal establishment] is the source of the first suggestions of the eventual use of every possible means, including military force, to contain Quebec and, if need be, to put her in her place.

Pierre Laporte's body was found in the trunk of a car at a small airport on the outskirts of Montreal on the night of October 17. James Cross was found alive in a small room in an apartment building in Montreal North on December 3, 1970. He told police that his abductors had been courteous and that he had not been mistreated. Five FLQ members were provided free passage to Cuba in exchange for Cross's release. Shortly after Christmas, FLQ members accused of the kidnapping and murder of Laporte were arrested.

There have been no other violent nationalist attacks in Quebec since the October crisis of 1970. Many politicians, including Trudeau, had no regrets about how the 1970 crisis was handled, because they believed that the end (WMA) justified the means. Yet, Jean Keable, the commissioner of an inquiry into illegal activities of the RCMP between 1970 and 1974, later said —

> Information that led to the resolution of the crisis was obtained by traditional investigation methods. The War Measures Act had not been necessary. However, this act did facilitate the arrests of many people and the ability to build a bank of information regarding Quebec nationalists, including the Parti Québécois, which was very useful to the RCMP during the years following the October crisis.

The FLQ crisis in October 1970 had a devastating effect on the Parti Québécois. In the spring of 1970, the PQ party had about 80,000 members. By autumn 1971, PQ membership had dropped to about 30,000. Lévesque realized that Quebeckers were having trouble differentiating between the various nationalist organizations. In April 1970, when the PQ won seven seats, the future of sovereignty-association had looked bright. In the aftermath of the October crisis, Lévesque would have to work hard to win back Quebeckers' support.

As the Parti Québécois began to rebuild following the October crisis, it had to come to terms with the unions. Some PQ members wanted the party to show more solidarity with the labour movement. Lévesque felt that it was better to keep union influence at arm's length.

In April 1972, the three predominant Quebec unions staged a general strike that paralyzed the province. About 200,000 public service employees went on strike simultaneously. Quebec was in chaos. Lévesque recalled —

The Common Front had closed the hospitals, not only closed them but mounted siege on them. I had seen Red Cross trucks stopped at "security" barriers and forced to turn back with their deliveries of plasma. Maintenance workers too, and visitors begging passes to see sick relatives.

The strikers were ordered back to work by the courts. When union leaders defied the court order, they were sent to a minimum-security institution for three months.

Claude Morin joined the Parti Québécois in May 1972. Morin, a former professor and the minister responsible for federal-provincial relations for two successive Liberal governments, brought a new twist to the strategy for achieving Quebec sovereignty. His controversial plan provoked a noisy two-year debate within the party.

In 1968, when the PQ was created, Lévesque had unequivocally stated that if the PQ was elected, Quebec sovereignty would be declared immediately afterwards. Morin introduced a step-by-step approach to sovereignty. Morin believed that it would be undemocratic to declare sovereignty immediately after coming to power. He said that if the PQ was elected, then it should hold a referendum on sovereignty in order to obtain the mandate of the Quebec people. After all, political parties sometimes form the government with less than 50 percent of the popular vote.

Militant members of the PQ were anxious because the separatism agenda wasn't moving fast enough and they were in danger of losing momentum. These members were concerned that a referendum on sovereignty was an unnecessary step that would bog down the movement.

Morin responded to this call for urgency with a poetic line: "Une fleur ne pousse pas plus vite parce-qu'on tire dessus" (a flower doesn't grow faster if you pull on it). Both Morin and Lévesque believed that a methodical approach was better in the long run because if Quebeckers felt that sovereignty was forced on them, the whole plan might backfire.

Apart from these internal policy dilemmas, the PQ also had to contend with federal espionage. In 1973, while the American public was preoccupied with the Watergate scandal, the Canadian RCMP was gathering information on PQ members through a well-established espionage campaign.

Between 1971 and 1978, police placed almost 600 concealed microphones in key locations throughout the province, including PQ headquarters and the homes of some PQ members. Then on January 9, 1973, a group of RCMP broke into the offices of Messageries Dynamiques, a courier company on Jeanne Mance Street, and stole the PQ membership list from a computer database.

Lévesque offset these tensions by putting aside the business of politics and going away for summer vacation. At least once a year, Lévesque and Corinne (usually accompanied by friends and Lévesque's sister, Alice) headed south to the beaches of Maine or Cape Cod. Lévesque took his relaxation as seriously as his work. By day, Lévesque liked to sunbathe and read. He took advantage of these rare opportunities to read for pleasure all day long. He read all sorts of books — science fiction, biographies, murder mysteries — almost anything except proposed legislation. Sometimes, he headed out to the shops in search of summer clothes and sandals.

Late afternoon would find Lévesque in the kitchen preparing hors d'oeuvres. He made appetizers with smoked salmon, Roquefort cheese, or anything else that went well with a martini. After a leisurely restaurant dinner, Lévesque and company settled down to all-night Scrabble games.

Meanwhile, Bourassa called an election for the end of October 1973. He was feeling confident because he had helped Quebec through the FLQ crisis as well as the union crisis, and unemployment levels were declining.

As the new election campaign revved up, Lévesque appeared to be more aware of his appearance. He began to wear a dapper navy blue suit and tie instead of an assortment of rumpled clothes, and he made an effort to put out his cigarette when he spotted a press photographer.

The PQ campaign went relatively well until October 9, when Lévesque released a budget that outlined the revenue and spending predictions of a PQ government during the first year of independence. Lévesque wanted to show Quebeckers that an independent Quebec would be more economical because there would not be any overlap of federal and provincial responsibilities. Parizeau proudly defended this hypothetical budget, which showed a surplus of $180 million despite a social affairs program that was equal to the current provincial budget.

This premature announcement of a sovereign Quebec's budget was probably not a good strategy because it was easy for the Liberal party to undermine PQ claims by simply stating that the figures were unrealistic. Bourassa stated that the federal government spent almost $7 million more in Quebec in 1971–1972 than they received from Quebec taxpayers. Then the PQ economists replied that the reverse was true — that Quebec taxpayers sent more money to Ottawa than they received in federal subsidies. Endless budget figures were bandied about by both Liberal and PQ politicians and the Quebec public grew more and more confused.

On October 29, Quebeckers went to the polls. A tidal wave of Liberal red swept across the province. Lévesque, who ran in the predominantly French-speaking riding of Dorion, did not win a seat. Also, prominent PQ Members of the National Assembly (MNA) — the new name for the provincial legislature — Camille Laurin and finance critic Guy Joron lost their seats. Now the PQ had a total of six seats, one seat less than in 1970.

Yet, incredibly, the PQ party did make some strides in 1973. Not only did they win almost a third of the popular vote, they were declared the official opposition. The PQ party gained the prestige (and the financial benefit) of opposition party status because their rivals — the Union Nationale and the Parti Créditiste — were slowly fading from the electoral landscape.

Lévesque knew that the PQ faithful were waiting for their leader to offer them some words of wisdom. After he composed himself, Lévesque made his way to the Paul Sauvé Arena. When he arrived, Camille Laurin latched on to him and cried on his shoulder like a baby. Lévesque was visibly uncomfortable with this outburst. He broke free of Laurin's embrace and strode onto the stage. The crowd had been waiting expectantly, and they listened with rapt attention when Lévesque stood tall and assured his followers, "One day, you can be sure, Quebec will overcome its last fears."

Lévesque was adept at putting on his public face and encouraging the PQ members to keep the faith. But privately, he was growing increasingly frustrated with his project for Quebec sovereignty. His ego was suffering after two electoral failures in three years. There was a great deal of internal discord regarding party strategy, and to top it all off — Lévesque was broke. Most of his parliamentary pension was going to his estranged wife and children, so Lévesque's only source of income was his column in *Le Journal de Montréal*. "I've done my part and now I'm going to hang up my skates," he confided to Corinne. He began to contemplate a return to full-time journalism.

But Lévesque's political colleagues would not let their leader leave so easily. Thousands of Quebeckers had jumped on the PQ bandwagon, and it simply wouldn't be fair for Lévesque to disappoint everyone at this point. One night, PQ colleagues, including Pierre Marois and Camille Laurin, met with Lévesque at his sister's house in Quebec City. His peers tried to encourage Lévesque by convincing him that he was the only one who could bring the Quebec sovereignty project to fruition. Pierre Marois recalled, "I was putting a lot of pressure on him that night, saying, 'You don't have the right [to quit now]' … what interrupted me was when I saw him starting to cry … I just had this realization that he is a human being and that maybe I had been pushing him too hard."

At the fifth PQ convention in November 1974, there was a heated debate about Claude Morin's step-by-step approach. There were three schools of thought on the matter: The *purs et durs* hard liners were completely against the idea of a referendum; Parizeau supporters wanted to take the pulse of the Quebec people by means of a poll and not a referendum; Lévesque and the other Morin supporters believed that a referendum on sovereignty was essential. Lévesque told conventioneers, "We are here to make Quebec a sovereign nation. But we want this transition to happen in a democratic and peaceful way with the rest of Canada. Without moving back at all, we would request, by means of a referendum, the support that we need to confirm the legitimacy of our mandate here and abroad."

The issue was voted on and the referendum option won two to one. The PQ party agreed that if negotiations with the federal government failed, then they would hold a referendum on sovereignty. Lévesque was pleased that a majority of PQ members had adopted the moderate approach, which would likely appeal to voters. Conventioneers who had voted against the plan shouted out their displeasure and then tore up their PQ membership cards in disgust.

There was so much infighting and tension within the PQ party that in September 1976, Lévesque decided to invite the PQ executive and the parliamentary wing to a meeting at the Auberge Handfield in Saint-Marc-sur-Richelieu, a small town east of Montreal. Before the meeting, Lévesque went for a walk by himself along the Richelieu River and through the inn's gardens to build up his strength for a confrontation. He knew that some members were openly questioning his authority. Lévesque entered the meeting room (late) with a coffee in one hand and a cigarette hanging from his mouth.

MNAs Charron and Burns were resentful because Lévesque never came to Quebec City for the weekly meetings to plan strategy. Not only was he not present, sometimes he even took a different position than them in his *Journal de Montréal* column. Guy Bisaillon commented, "If there are factions in the PQ, [Monsieur] Lévesque is responsible … the PQ is a coalition party but the balance between opposing views is no longer assured. It's always the same ones who have to water down their ideas. I think that we need someone else at the head of the party."

Corinne stared nervously out the window. It looked like Lévesque's meeting was turning into a *putsch*. Then Burns added, "Our problem is leadership. René says that there is no team spirit in the PQ. It's true, but it's because there is no leader."

Then a moderate PQ member shouted out, "Nobody here can replace Mr. Lévesque!"

Emboldened by this vote of confidence, Lévesque made a declaration. He banged the table with his fist and bellowed at the dissident members, "If you want my head, come and get it at the convention! We will see who will be the leader!"

But Bourassa called an election before the next PQ convention. As the PQ members rallied to prepare another election campaign, they may have wondered whether Bourassa knew that he had unwittingly saved the PQ party and its leader — René Lévesque.

Chapter 8
Premier
René Lévesque

The election was called for November 15, 1976. Lévesque was surprised that Bourassa was calling an election two years before his mandate expired, at a time when his political standing was weak. There was widespread dissatisfaction with overspending on the Montreal 1976 Olympics and the James Bay hydroelectric project, as well as accusations of political patronage. However, the main issue for many English-speaking Quebeckers (a vital component of the Liberal party's base) was Bill 22 — a law that proclaimed French to be the official language of Quebec.

In the fall of 1976, the PQ promised Quebeckers the sun, the moon, and the stars. Their ambitious platform comprised: creating a more transparent and democratic government, progressive social measures, such as free public daycare, and boosting the economy by supporting small- and medium-sized companies. The PQ also promised to establish a public library and a *maison de la culture* (cultural centre) in every municipality.

The PQ consciously emphasized their ambitious socio-economic agenda and put the sovereignty issue on the back burner. Whenever sovereignty-association was discussed, the referendum was mentioned in the same breath.

A month before the election, polls showed that 43 percent of Quebeckers supported the PQ. Although the PQ's future looked brighter than ever, Lévesque knew that he couldn't count on an easy win. The results of the last two elections had been disappointing in regard to both Lévesque's career and the PQ's political future.

The PQ began to line up its candidates for the 1976 election. Some candidates, such as Camille Laurin, remained faithful to their traditional ridings. While others, including Lévesque, shifted ridings to improve their odds of electoral victory. Lévesque's organizers recommended that their leader run in Taillon, a "sure" riding in the working class area of Longueuil on the south shore of Montreal. Everyone worried that Lévesque would not win his seat, including Corinne, who, the night before the election, dreamed that all of the PQ candidates were elected except Lévesque.

Many new faces graced this campaign, including Lise Payette, the feminist star of a popular Radio-Canada program; Gérald Godin, a journalist and poet; and Yves Bérubé, an engineer from the Gaspé. In a fascinating twist of history, the sons of two former Union Nationale leaders, Pierre-Marc Johnson and Jean-François Bertrand, also ran under the PQ banner.

Lévesque knew that some polls predicted a PQ victory and the fact that the Sureté de Québec (provincial police) had recently assigned bodyguards to protect him was a good omen. Yet, Lévesque did not permit himself to feel overly optimistic. He knew that Quebeckers were quite conservative and that they might decide to overlook most of Bourassa's shortcomings and vote him back into power. At one point, Lévesque said, "It would be black magic if the PQ were able to overturn a Liberal majority of 100 MNAs."

Then the impossible happened. On a cold and cloudy morning in mid-November 1976, 85 percent of the registered voters from the Gaspé to the Outaouis came out to vote, and an awful lot of them took a chance on a revolutionary party and its charismatic leader.

Lévesque watched the announcement of election results on television at an apartment above the Taillon riding office. While frantically chain-smoking, Lévesque was heard to mutter, "C'est pas possible! C'est pas possible!" (It's not possible!) At 8:40 p.m., the television announcer stated that the Parti Québécois would be forming a majority government, and Lévesque (who had finally won a seat) would be the new premier.

Lévesque was stunned. The victory had come almost too fast. By the time the recount was complete, there were 71 Parti Québécois MNAs. A crowd of thousands gathered at Paul Sauvé Arena to greet Lévesque and the newly elected MNAs. Quebeckers were overcome with emotion; they were clapping, shouting, and weeping with joy. A sea of people began to sing Gilles Vigneault's nationalist refrain: "Gens du pays, c'est votre tour, de vous laisser parler d'amour ..." (Countrymen, now it's your turn, to let yourselves speak of love.) Earlier that night, an ecstatic Camille Laurin had urged Quebeckers to dance in the streets; they finally had a government for which they had waited more than 200 years.

When Lévesque finally arrived, the crowd roared with pleasure. According to one of Lévesque's assistants, "It was utter madness. He [Lévesque] did not touch the floor all night. His bodyguards were overwhelmed. I thought that he would not get out of there alive."

Lévesque had two sets of notes for his speech on that historic night. He planned on using the first set if the PQ won about 15 seats; he would use the second set if the PQ won about 30 seats. He was not prepared for a "miracle." He began —

> We are not a little people. We are perhaps something like a great people. Never in my life did I think that I would be so proud to be a Quebecker. We hoped for the victory of our party and we wished for it with all our heart. But we never

thought that it would happen like this, already this year. Politically, it is the most beautiful and the greatest night in Quebec history ...

Outside, Quebeckers waved fleur-du-lis flags from their cars and honked as they drove along Montreal's major streets. The celebration continued into the wee hours of the morning.

Félix Leclerc, a revered Quebec poet and *chansonnier*, wrote a ballad to commemorate this historic night ...

Ne mettez pas de mots
Laissez tonner de joie
Six millions de poitrines
Six millions de saluts
Sur les deux bords du fleuve
À partir d'aujourd'hui
On bâtit, on bâtit

(Don't use any words ... Let the joy thunder ... Six million beating hearts ... Six million greetings ... On both sides of the (St. Lawrence) River ... Starting today, we are building ... We are building)

On the day after the election, everyone was happy to note that the proverbial sky had not fallen: the value of the Canadian dollar had only quivered, the share prices of major Quebec companies were stable, and Quebec savings bond sales were not dramatically different than usual. The next step was to form the Cabinet, a process that Lévesque referred to as "Penelope's weaving." Like the character in Homer's *Odyssey* who was continually undoing her work and starting afresh, Lévesque felt caught up in a never-ending process.

Lévesque invited his best and brightest to a meeting at the Hatley Inn in the Eastern Townships. He realized that now he was in the same position that Lesage had been in 1960 — most of his potential Cabinet ministers were political neophytes. Jacques Parizeau and Claude Morin were former civil servants, but the rest of the crew were bright, enthusiastic, and absolutely inexperienced. While there were no representatives from the business world in his collection of new MNAs, there was abundant representation from academia, journalism, and law. Lévesque, the law school drop-out, was amazed that he would be leading a group of people who had earned their doctorates at top universities in the United States and Europe. He wondered if he would "be able to keep charge of the helm, when the crew is made up of so many potential captains."

Lévesque worked hard to strike a balance between fresh new faces and the old PQ faithful, while trying to incorporate geographic representation. One of Lévesque's advisers suggested that Lévesque adopt a modified version of the

Ontario provincial government's super-ministries. This extra level of ministers above the Cabinet was supposed to help the government set priorities. After Lévesque named his Cabinet ministers, he chose five new ministers of state to co-ordinate economic development, cultural development, regional development, social development, and parliamentary reform.

On December 14, 1976, Quebec's first separatist government was inaugurated. There were a few symbolic breaks with tradition: the speaker wore a suit instead of robes; there was a moment of silence instead of a prayer; and the inaugural address was read in French only. This bold introduction resonated across Canada.

The PQ's first term got off to a rocky start. Before the PQ could get down to business, they had to clean up a financial mess left behind by Bourassa — the $1.2 billion Olympic deficit — three times more than the estimated cost.

Then in late January, Lévesque fell flat on his face at the Economic Club of New York. This elite association of American financiers had invited Lévesque to explain his plans for the future. There was a lot at stake: trade between Quebec and the United States was worth about $8 billion. Lévesque's economic adviser wrote the first draft of the speech, which was entitled "Quebec: a Good Neighbour in Transition." Then Lévesque and a few other colleagues fine-tuned it. Lévesque began by telling the audience that the new Quebec government "was born of a young political party that had gained strength during the two previous elections, with political sovereignty as its main objective." He sensed that the financiers weren't very receptive to this idea, but he carried on with the prepared speech. "A new nation is developing north of your border, the way yours did two hundred years ago. We can no longer continue to be a hostage of the Canadian constitution," said Lévesque.

The American investors did not see the parallel between the American Revolution and Lévesque's nationalist plans. In fact, they were insulted that Lévesque compared the Americans' rebellion against British colonial oppressors to the removal of a Canadian province from Ottawa's benign federal government. Ultimately, Lévesque's speech focused more on Quebec separation than on concrete financial information. The investors were not reassured. Lévesque was disappointed, too. He blamed part of the failure on the fact that he had followed a prepared speech. He normally improvised his speeches from a set of notes, in order to have more flexibility.

More trouble occurred a few weeks later. In February, less than three months after the election victory, Lévesque was involved in a tragic car accident. One Saturday night, he, Corinne, and a couple of friends were invited to dinner at Yves and Monique Michaud's house in the Côte-des-Neiges neighbourhood, northwest of downtown Montreal. Yves was a wine connoisseur, so there were several very special bottles of wine on the table. By the time dinner was over, Lévesque had consumed about five glasses of wine and a few sips of pear liqueur. At 4 a.m. Sunday, he and Corinne prepared to leave. Lévesque downed a few cups of coffee before heading out. There was no traffic in the middle of the night, so the couple zoomed down Côte-des-Neiges in their vermilion Ford Capri (Lévesque did not use a chauffeur on weekends).

Near the corner of Cedar, a man was frantically waving his arms. Lévesque did not slow down or stop to see what was the matter. Instead, he accelerated the car and swerved left to avoid hitting the man. Then Corinne saw a body lying in the middle of the street. They were going too fast to stop. Lévesque hit the body and dragged it for 30 metres. The premier of Quebec had just killed a 62-year-old homeless man named Edgar Trottier.

Police arrived on the scene right away. They did not perform a breathalyzer test because they believed Lévesque to be distressed, not drunk.

The next day, Lévesque's friends and colleagues were shocked to learn about the accident. His closest friends frequently worried that he might be involved in a car accident because of his habit of not wearing glasses when he drove (even though this driver's license stipulated that they were necessary), and he was often distracted.

The police report stated that Lévesque was not responsible for the death of Edgar Trottier. Far from demanding his resignation, the adoring Quebec public was sympathetic to Lévesque's situation. His popularity barely faltered.

Chapter 9
Reshaping Quebec Society

uring their first mandate, the PQ brought in some progressive socio-economic legislation. Lévesque's proudest moment was the ratification of a law regulating political party fundraising. He had long said that if he were elected, he would clean up party financing. Skeptics had snidely told him that it was easy to be virtuous when you're not in power. Lévesque was determined to prove them wrong and put an end to Quebec's slush-fund tradition.

Robert Burns, Minister of State for Parliamentary Reform, tabled the PQ's revolutionary election-financing legislation. It was the most rigorous legislation of its kind in the western world. The main tenets of this bill were: provincial political parties had to make their financial statements public; contributions to a political party could not come from companies or lobby groups; no contributor could give more than $3000 in one year, and gifts worth more than $100 had to be declared.

Naturally, there weren't too many objectors to a law that upheld democratic principles. However, two other significant pieces of legislation from the PQ's first term — a law regulating language and another regarding automobile insurance — provoked veritable storms of dissension.

Quebeckers were frustrated with their automobile insurance system. Automobile insurance premiums were higher in Quebec than anywhere else in Canada. In 1977, a 25-year-old single male, driving a current model, paid $1800 a year for car insurance, assuming he could find a company to insure him. As a result, many Quebeckers chose not to purchase car insurance. When the PQ came to power, about 20 percent of vehicles on the road were not insured.

Automobile insurance reform, a PQ electoral promise, landed in Lise Payette's lap because she was the minister of Consumers, Co-operatives, and Financial Institutions. Payette, a former television host, dove into the file and soon became an automobile insurance expert. She and her team developed a new insurance plan that ensured that all victims of car accidents were compensated. There were two basic components: a government-operated no-fault insurance coverage for personal injuries and mandatory private insurance coverage for material damage. Payette had to convince the Cabinet that the proposed insurance plan was tenable. Then she had to convince lawyers, insurance agents, and other people with vested interests in the status quo. This law was heralded as one of the most important laws of the PQ's first mandate.

The law that caused the most friction was Camille Laurin's *Charte de la Langue Française*, also known as Bill 101. During the 1976 election campaign, the PQ had promised to abolish mandatory English tests that were required for entrance to English schools under Bill 22. Shortly after the Cabinet was formed, Lévesque asked Camille Laurin to modify the Liberal government's unpopular language law. Laurin, a tireless worker, went much further than Lévesque anticipated. His proposed *Charte de la Langue Française* comprised 225 articles.

Laurin was an earnest and indefatigable man. Before joining the nascent PQ party, Laurin had been medical director of the Albert Prévost Psychiatric Institute. Despite tremendous opposition, Laurin had transformed the psychiatric hospital from a degrading prison for the mentally ill to a centre that delivered modern psychiatric care. Now Laurin wanted to employ his psychiatric training to help French Quebeckers regain their sense of identity. Bolstering the French language was the key to recovery. To Laurin, the *Charte de la Langue Française* wasn't just proposed legislation, it was psychotherapy. Laurin strongly believed that French should be the only language used in public administration, the courts, and in the workplace. He also believed the English school system to be completely unnecessary.

In 1976, English-speaking voters had deserted the Liberal party in droves because they were unhappy with Bill 22. Yet Laurin's charter would have far more dramatic impact on the linguistic landscape. Lévesque did not appreciate Laurin's blunt perspective, and he had many run-ins with Laurin, whom he described as having the "softness of steel." Lévesque preferred to walk the moderate line. Although he wanted to protect the French language, he did not want to risk abusing the civil rights of minority groups.

However, Laurin and Lévesque did see eye to eye on one major language issue — they both believed that children of immigrants should attend French schools. They believed that if immigrants were allowed to choose the language of education for their children, a decline in the percentage of Francophones in Quebec would be inevitable.

The rights of English-speaking families were a different matter. The *Charte de la Langue Française* stated that only those children with at least one parent who had studied in English in Quebec would be permitted to attend English schools. Laurin believed that Canadians from other provinces should be treated like immigrants from anywhere else in the world. Lévesque was uncomfortable with Laurin's hardline position. He believed that the children of Anglophones who moved to Quebec from another part of Canada should be allowed to send their children to English schools.

There was much debate within the Cabinet regarding the education articles of the charter and an article that stated that all commercial signage in Quebec should be in French only. Some ministers worried that the signage article would precipitate the departure of corporate head offices.

Ultimately, some corporations did decide to relocate, including the Sun Life Insurance Company. At the beginning of 1978, Sun Life left its grand Beaux-Arts Building (once the tallest building in the British Commonwealth) on Dominion Square and moved its headquarters to Toronto. The departure of this company — a symbol of English elite power — was highly publicized.

Sun Life president, Thomas Galt, explained that Bill 101 had threatened to interfere with "the recruitment and maintenance of competent employees possessing the knowledge of English required for the daily operation of the company." Lévesque shed crocodile tears on hearing of their departure because, as far as he was concerned, Sun Life had never been an integral part of Quebec society. Galt did not speak a word of French, almost 80 percent of the employees were unilingual Anglophones, and most of Sun Life's investments were in companies outside of Quebec.

Some media sources claimed that 91 corporate head offices had left Quebec since the PQ victory. This was a gross exaggeration, as many of these "corporations" were numbered companies that existed only on paper.

In late August, the provincial premiers gathered at

St. Andrews by-the–Sea, New Brunswick, for a little lobster, a little sea air, and a lot of heated debate. Lévesque knew that many of the premiers were uncomfortable with Bill 101, so he decided to sweeten the medicine with a reciprocity clause. This clause would ensure that provinces that enabled their French-speaking minority population to study in French would have the favour returned (that is, Anglophones from those provinces who moved to Quebec would be allowed to educate their children in English).

The conference host, Premier Richard Hatfield, was a fervent believer in bilingualism. He worried that acceptance of the reciprocity clause would be a tacit approval of uni-lingualism in Quebec. Hatfield and the other premiers were interested in a general discussion about the improvement of minority language education, however, they didn't really want to discuss the reciprocity proposal. Lévesque was hurt by the premiers' indifference.

On August 26, 1977, Bill 101 was passed. The Quebec national assembly had spent most of the summer debating its various articles — a total of 36 sessions — and more than 217 hours. Laurin was triumphant that he had "saved" the French language in Quebec.

About a week after Bill 101 came into effect, Prime Minister Trudeau informed the premiers that he was ready to amend the constitution to include language rights regarding education. Francophones in provinces outside of Quebec would have the right to a French education if the size of the population justified it. Lévesque rejected Trudeau's proposal immediately, because he was concerned that if language of education was incorporated into the constitution, then Quebec would lose its provincial right to govern education.

In November, Lévesque embarked on an official visit to France. After visiting Charles de Gaulle's tomb in the Lorraine region, he flew to Paris. The French government rolled out the red carpet for Lévesque and welcomed him as if he were a head of state. Lévesque was overwhelmed by the level of excitement generated by his visit. Gérard Pelletier, the Canadian ambassador to France, was not amused.

The mayor of Paris, Jacques Chirac, hosted a magnificent reception for Lévesque at l'Hôtel de ville. Some blue-and-white Quebec flags had been put up amid the elaborate gilded furniture and chandeliers in the city hall's formal rooms. Chirac was supportive of Lévesque's sovereignty-association plans. He expressed surprise that a "nation" as wealthy and as progressive as Quebec was not already independent. Lévesque was the darling of the Paris media. Journalists commented on how refreshing it was to interview an unpretentious down-to-earth politician.

Following the city hall reception, Lévesque was hosted by the French president, Valéry Giscard d'Estaing. D'Estaing, who had once taught at a private French school in the elite Montreal neighbourhood of Outremont, was interested in Lévesque's ideas. However, he was not as overtly enthusiastic as Chirac. In a closing speech, d'Estaing explained that

France did not want to become involved in the domestic dispute between Canada and Quebec. France valued its special relationship with Quebec and it would maintain this relationship, regardless of Quebec's status vis-à-vis Canada. D'Estaing did not refer to Quebec sovereignty during his speech, although he concluded with a high-charged quote from Gilles Vigneault's song "Mon Pays" — "Si long que soit l'hiver, le printemps un jour lui succède." (No matter how long winter is — spring always follows.)

Before leaving France, Lévesque agreed to meet with the French Prime Minister, Raymond Barre, on an annual basis in either Quebec City or Paris. This was a bit unusual, considering that Lévesque and Barre were not political equals. Barre was the prime minister of a sovereign country, while Lévesque was the premier of a province within a sovereign country.

Back at home, the PQ's first mandate was marked by several squabbles with the federal government regarding jurisdiction. One of the most heated conflicts was about sales tax. The Canadian economy was floundering in the late winter and early spring of 1978. In April, Jean Chrétien, the federal Minister of Finance, asked the provinces to lower their sales tax by three percent for a period of six months, in order to help fight inflation and to stimulate the economy. Ottawa promised to reimburse the provinces two-thirds of the lost revenue.

Parizeau, who was minister of Finance, minister of Revenue, and president of the Treasury Board, didn't know which way to turn. He didn't want to kowtow to the federal government regarding the sales tax cuts plan because sales tax is provincial jurisdiction. On the other hand, he didn't want to miss out on $226 million in compensation. So, Quebec responded with its own plan. It would eliminate sales tax from the products of vulnerable Quebec industries, including furniture production and shoe manufacturing, for a period of two years and leave the sales tax on all other items. Lévesque's financial wizard sat back and waited for the federal compensation to arrive.

But Jean Chrétien was a proud man who was not interested in negotiating. He did not appreciate the way that Parizeau had transformed an across-the-board sales tax cut into a means to boost weak Quebec industries. So he told Quebec that if it did not step in line with the provinces that were prepared to follow the federal plan, then it would not be entitled to a reimbursement. He wanted to penalize the Quebec government for not co-operating, although he knew that there would be an outcry if Quebec was the only province that was not reimbursed. Finally, Chrétien decided to send $85 to each Québecker as an income-tax rebate.

This new twist upset Parizeau because the reimbursement sum was owed to the Quebec government and not to individuals. Parizeau was left wondering how the government was going to recoup this money without making Quebeckers feel that they were being denied their "little gift" from the federal government.

Chapter 10
The End of a Dream

Militants in the PQ party were chomping at the bit to begin planning the referendum. For many members, this had been their main concern since the PQ came to power. But it wouldn't be easy. As soon as the PQ began planning the referendum strategy, party division surfaced.

In October 1978, Lévesque told the National Assembly, "We have no intention of first obtaining sovereignty and then negotiating an association." He continued, "We do not want to end, but rather to radically transform our union with the rest of Canada, so that, in the future, our relations will be based on full and complete equality."

For the more militant members of the PQ, who would have been more than happy to remove the hyphen linking sovereignty and association, Lévesque's latest position seemed weaker than ever. They had jumped on Lévesque's bandwagon because they believed in Quebec sovereignty and now it looked like Quebec sovereignty was more dependent on successful negotiations with Canada than on the desires of Quebeckers.

At the beginning of 1979, the Pepin-Robarts Task Force on Canadian Unity submitted their report to Trudeau. This bold report reflected some of Lévesque's age-old requests. It stated that Quebec should have the right to self-determination and that the constitution should recognize Quebec's distinctiveness. The Pepin-Robarts Report also recommended that the provinces be given the right to control language policy and to exert more power over social and cultural affairs. This was not what Trudeau was waiting to hear. The prime minister dismissed the report, even though his government had commissioned it.

Things seemed to be going from bad to worse, and Lévesque was finding it difficult to maintain an optimistic perspective. One of the few bright lights in the spring of 1979 was that Lévesque finally married Corinne. After living together for 10 years, Corinne no longer expected Lévesque to pop the question. Lévesque overcame his wariness of the institution of marriage (he was, by this time, divorced from Louise) to celebrate his love with Corinne; and also because Corinne's ambivalent status at official functions was creating some embarrassing situations. The simple civil ceremony took place in mid-April at the Palais de Justice, witnessed by only Corinne's father and Lévesque's brother-in-law.

Trudeau and Lévesque were playing a waiting game. Trudeau was waiting for Lévesque to call a referendum and Lévesque was waiting for Trudeau to call a federal election. They were both waiting for the other to lose support. Trudeau lost first. There was a federal election on May 22, 1979, and Joe Clark was voted in as the new prime minister of Canada. Lévesque felt that Clark was more open to discussion with Quebec than Trudeau, so it seemed like the perfect opportunity for the PQ to hold their referendum. It was not meant to be. Clark's government fell, due to a non-confidence vote on a new budget, after only about six months in power.

After months of discussion, the wording of the referendum question reached a climax during an intense all-night meeting on December 19. Lévesque wanted the referendum question to ask Quebeckers for a mandate to negotiate sovereignty-association, as opposed to asking Quebeckers to adopt sovereignty-association immediately. This strategy necessitated another referendum to vote on the negotiation results. Some PQ members were pulling their hair out at the plodding pace of the process, but Lévesque was mainly concerned with formulating a referendum question that was transparent and fair. Lévesque and his 25 ministers worked all night, changing one word at a time, until everyone's nerves were frayed. One participant wondered aloud whether it was a question or a book. At one o'clock in the morning, the government's top legal minds reviewed the document. Finally, on December 20, Lévesque announced the referendum question —

> The Government of Quebec has made public its proposal to negotiate a new agreement with the rest of Canada, based on the equality of nations; this agreement would enable Quebec to acquire the exclusive power to make its laws, levy its taxes, and establish relations abroad — in other words, sovereignty — and at the same time, to maintain with Canada an economic association including a common currency; any change in political status resulting from these negotiations will be submitted to you the people through a referendum; on these terms, do you give the Government of Quebec the mandate to negotiate the proposed agreement between Quebec and Canada?

Claude Ryan, leader of the provincial Liberals, and his team began to mount a political campaign to oppose the referendum question — the *non* campaign. Then Trudeau was re-elected in February 1980 and the political landscape shifted again. Trudeau and his advisers worried about the Liberals' weak response to the PQ's articulate and well-rehearsed arguments in the National Assembly. They had no confidence in Ryan's low-key, hand-shaking style of campaign, and they did not like Ryan's campaign slogan "Mon

Non est Québécois" (a play on words meaning that both my name and my "no" vote are Québécois).

Ultimately, the federal government played a significant role in developing and executing the "non" campaign strategy. Ryan resented the arrival of Ottawa's "big guns," and he vetoed any campaign concept that came from the federal government.

At the beginning of March, Lise Payette, now the minister of state for the Status of Women, paid a significant political price for inadvertently insulting Claude Ryan's wife. At a regional PQ meeting, Payette tried to explain why she didn't like Ryan's approach. She worried that he wanted Quebec women to be submissive like "Yvette" (a submissive and obsequious character in a primary school reader). Then Payette added that Ryan was married to an "Yvette." It was a strangely sexist comment from a minister who was supposed to advance the feminist cause.

A month later, 15,000 proud homemakers and self-described "Yvettes" filled the Montreal forum. Each one waved the Quebec flag in one hand and the Canadian flag in the other. There were dozens of speeches by prominent Quebeckers and a media circus recorded the event. Liberal organizers had engineered a real coup for the "non" campaign.

Trudeau arrived late on the scene for the referendum campaign, but he wasn't too late. He made four articulate and persuasive speeches for the "non" campaign, which put him squarely back in the director's chair.

In the meantime, Lévesque traversed the province, making hundreds of speeches for the "oui" campaign. At some
gatherings he gave out certificates to regional or professional
groups who were dedicated to the "oui" movement, while the
campaign tune, "*Oui, c'est parti*," played in the background.

Yet, despite the large and enthusiastic audiences that
Lévesque attracted, he began to sense that the majority of the
Quebec population still wasn't ready to take a chance. The
"oui" campaign was counting on the support of 10 percent
of Quebec's non-Francophones. To win the referendum, 62
percent of Quebec's French-speaking population had to vote
"oui," and Lévesque was not confident that they could count
on that happening.

On May 20, 1980, a beautiful spring day, a record 86 per-
cent of Quebeckers exercised their democratic right to vote.
Around midday, Lévesque voted at Saint Patrick's Church on
Dorchester Boulevard (now called Boulevard René Lévesque).

That night, a crowd of 5000 people gathered at the Paul
Sauvé Arena. With great anticipation, they waited for the
referendum results to come in. Some people in the crowd
reminisced about how they had experienced the same feeling
of nervous energy four years earlier. This time, there would
be no miracle. Three-fifths of Quebeckers voted against the
mandate to negotiate sovereignty-association.

Pauline Julien performed a song "for healing" while
the crowd wept. Finally, Lévesque arrived with Corinne and
Lise Payette, who were both dressed like they were going to

a funeral. The crowd greeted Lévesque with a standing ovation that seemed to have a life of its own. Even Lévesque had trouble getting the crowd to quiet. Once the applauding and chanting subsided, Lévesque gave his loyal supporters a glimmer of hope. He said, "If I have understood you properly, you are saying, 'Wait until next time'." After his concession speech, Lévesque left the crowd with a heartfelt "À la prochaine!" (Until the next time!)

Lévesque did not fully express himself on that emotionally draining night. He was genuinely hurt that a majority of Quebeckers had lacked the confidence to take a leap of faith with him. In his memoirs, he pondered, "How many people are there in the world who have refused such a chance to acquire full powers for themselves peacefully and democratically?"

Less than a year after the referendum, there was a provincial election. The PQ was voted back into office with a comfortable majority on April 13, 1981. But the second term had none of the optimism and excitement of the first term. Everything began to fall apart. It was a time of loss and despair.

One of Lévesque's first disappointments in the second mandate was the course of constitutional negotiations. For years, Pierre Trudeau had been talking about repatriating the constitution. The provincial premiers were not opposed to the principle of repatriation, but they were concerned about Trudeau's autocratic methods. Provincial premiers had already met countless times to discuss amending formulas (criteria required for changing an article of the constitution) and

René Lévesque suffers defeat in the 1980 Quebec referendum.

whether or not to comply with Trudeau's desire to incorporate the Charter of Rights and Freedoms into the constitution.

In November 1981, Trudeau summoned the premiers for yet one more constitutional negotiation. There was a sense that this time would either make it or break it. Most of the provincial delegations took suites at the sumptuous Château Laurier Hotel, which is conveniently located across the street from the conference centre. However, the Quebec delegation set up camp at the Plaza de la Chaudière across the river in Hull. When talks began, Premier William Davis of Ontario and Premier Richard Hatfield of New Brunswick agreed with Trudeau's plans to repatriate and to amend the constitution. However,

Quebec and the seven other provinces (the Gang of Eight) were opposed to Trudeau's plans for unilateral patriation.

On November 4, Trudeau came up with a new proposal. He suggested repatriating the constitution first and then putting a moratorium on discussions regarding the amending formula and the Charter of Rights. If no agreement were reached after two years, there would be a national referendum.

Some of the English Canadian premiers viewed a referendum as foreign to the parliamentary system. As all the premiers were trying to come to terms with this concept, Trudeau encouraged Lévesque to get him on board. "You're the great democrat, the great believer in referendums," he said.

Some premiers indicated that they might accept this new proposal and the Quebec delegation realized that if the Gang of Eight dissolved, they would be in a very vulnerable position. They knew that it was better to take a chance on the future than risk an immediate loss.

When Lévesque arrived for a planned breakfast meeting the next morning, Brian Peckford, premier of Newfoundland, told him that the new proposal was next to his plate. The other premiers had stayed up all night drafting a new package, and Quebec had been left out of the discussion.

Lévesque was floored. He had no intention of signing the new agreement because there were so many clauses that he objected to, such as the minority language rights clause in the Charter of Rights, which would override Bill 101. Lévesque also objected to the removal of the financial compensation clause for opting out of national programs. The worst aspect of this situation was Lévesque's keen sense of betrayal and humiliation. After spending most of his adult life trying to strengthen Quebec's position, Quebec was now in a weaker position. There was no longer any hope that Canada would recognize Quebec's special status.

Later that day, a dejected and battered Lévesque boarded the Quebec government's F-27 jet at Gatineau Airport to fly home. Lévesque had just been dealt a blow from which he would never recover. His sense of betrayal was palpable when he referred to the constitutional settlement as the "night of the long knives" (a reference to a night in 1934 when Adolf Hitler exterminated hundreds of his potential political rivals).

At the outset of the December PQ convention, party members shared a sense of anger and frustration about the constitutional settlement. However, their visions of the political future were diverging. Some members wanted to abandon the step-by-step approach to sovereignty-association. They favoured achieving independence. And they wanted the next election to be a referendum. Lévesque had dealt with this extreme position before. In fact, he had spent most of his political career trying to keep the militant faction of the PQ in check, so the party would appeal to the electorate. Would he be able to control the militants' impatience one more time?

When it was time for PQ members to vote on hundreds of proposed changes to the party program, Lévesque shifted in his seat. As they approached the resolution that proposed eliminating the word "association" from the party program, Lévesque must have wondered whether he was dreaming. He reminded conventioneers that the interdependence of Quebec and Canada was deeply entrenched, and that if they adopted a hard-line policy, the party's future would be at stake. But many PQ members were not convinced. One delegate shouted out, "It would be masochistic, even obscene, to suggest an association now, after what has just happened!"

Finally, party members voted in favour of the resolution, effectively stating their goal as independence and not sovereignty-association. It looked like the PQ party was going to adopt a hard-line position like the former RIN party.

Then, a man with long, red hair rushed up to the microphone. Jacques Rose wanted to comment on a motion that imprisoned former FLQ members, including his brother Paul, be transferred to Quebec prisons. Jacques had been convicted as an accessory to the kidnapping, and his brother Paul had been convicted of Pierre Laporte's murder. When Rose received a wild ovation and was praised as a "pioneer for the liberation of Quebec," Lévesque felt the philosophy of the PQ fundamentally change. At the end of the convention, Lévesque told the PQ, "If I put myself in the voter's shoes, I would have some difficulty in voting for me under these conditions!"

Apart from this internal party conflict, Lévesque also had to face a dire financial situation that led to a nasty confrontation with the unions. In the latter part of 1981 and 1982, the whole country was gripped by an economic recession and skyrocketing unemployment. Quebec was hit even harder than other provinces — 44 percent of the jobs lost in Canada were in Quebec. Parizeau's expansionist budget and a generous pre-referendum settlement with the Common Front (Quebec's three predominant unions) had tipped Quebec over a financial precipice. The PQ government was short $700 million, and it was about to go bankrupt. Lévesque was sure that he could convince the unions to sacrifice some of their promised salary increases to help the province get back on its feet. He was wrong. The unions did not budge.

At this point, Parizeau devised a financial solution in which the PQ gave to public service employees with one hand and took away with the other. When the unions discovered that salary cutbacks had been legislated before any negotiation was possible, they were outraged. There were escalating strikes by different groups, including teachers and hospital workers, beginning in January 1983. On January 29, almost 30,000 public sector employees marched in Quebec City. Many of the strikers felt betrayed by the Parti Québécois, which had arrived on the political scene as a left-wing, pro-labour movement.

The strikers' surprise turned to shock in February when the National Assembly approved draconian back-to-work legislation. Bill 111 threatened the public service employees with salary loss, seniority loss, firings without recourse or appeal and — incredibly — suspension of the provincial and the federal charters of rights. Where was the passionate humanitarian who had been outraged by the loss of civil rights in 1970 under the War Measures Act?

Lévesque had always had two very different aspects to his personality. At times, he was witty, tolerant, and open-minded. But he also had a dark side, a distant and suspicious alter ego. In the fall of 1984, Lévesque's dark side took precedence. The disappointments and frustrations of the last couple of years had taken their toll. Lévesque's friends and colleagues watched in shock as he began to fall apart before their eyes. He was having trouble analyzing issues and making decisions. He couldn't help the Cabinet achieve consensus. And the great orator, who was renowned for moving and persuasive speeches, was now stumbling on his words. Lévesque was suffering from serious depression.

Meanwhile, his loss of confidence in the sovereignty option had provoked open revolt among a group of Cabinet ministers. In October 1984, Jacques Léonard, the minister of Transport, organized a meeting at his farm in the Laurentians. Camille Laurin, Gilbert Paquette, Denise Leblanc-Bantey, Louise Harel, Marcel Léger, and Robert Dean joined Léonard to discuss the promotion of Quebec independence and to ensure that the next election was about sovereignty. These ministers believed that their leader, Lévesque, was losing sight of his goal.

Lévesque thought that he was just being realistic. If the majority of Quebeckers did not want to hear any more about sovereignty or referendums for the time being, then maybe it was better to put these ideas "on ice." On November 19, 1984, Lévesque declared, "We must surely resign ourselves, in my humble opinion, to the fact that sovereignty must not be at stake: neither in whole nor in more or less disguised parts."

Dissident ministers (referred to as The Group of 12) were astounded to learn that the man who had inspired them to work towards Quebec independence was giving up on the dream. Pierre Marois, one of Lévesque's closest supporters, had warned him in June of 1983 that some ministers were likely to resign. Lévesque had confidently replied, "Ministers don't quit."

Lévesque discovered to his chagrin that ministers do quit. On November 21, 1984, Jacques Parizeau, Jacques Léonard, Camille Laurin, Denise Leblanc-Bantey, and Gilbert Paquette resigned from the Cabinet. A few days later, Louise Harel resigned from her ministerial position. Around the same time, several MNAs decided to leave the caucus and sit as independents.

On January 10, 1985, Lévesque was in his office with his colleagues Louis Bernard, Pierre-Marc Johnson, and Bernard Landry. They were very concerned about their leader's mental state, so they suggested that the premier take a break or perhaps consult a doctor. Lévesque became increasingly exasperated with these suggestions, and he exploded with rage. Then he punched Louis Bernard.

Lévesque's friends and colleagues knew that this

violent man was not the René Lévesque they had once known. He wasn't just tired, he was sick. A doctor was summoned. Lévesque was administered a tranquilizer and sent to hospital. One colleague who witnessed this sad moment in Lévesque's life felt that he was watching an injured lion being carted off. The next day, Lévesque, who was deemed to be in good general health, was released.

On June 20, 1985, the last day of the spring session, there was a small celebration to mark the 25th anniversary of Lévesque's first election (June 22, 1960). Dozens of political colleagues paid tribute to him with flowery speeches. Lévesque did not appreciate all of these blatant hints for him to step down.

Although Lévesque had already decided that he was ready to hand the reigns of power to Pierre-Marc Johnson, he wanted to orchestrate his own departure. That evening, Lévesque officially resigned from the leadership of the Parti Québécois.

Lévesque, who had never been interested in the trappings of power, had lived very simply in Quebec City at 91 bis, d'Auteuil Street. When Lévesque's landlady, Francine Jolicoeur, offered to drive him to the train station after his retirement from politics, she was amazed by his lack of material possessions — "This man, who had given birth to a political movement, arrived with nothing and left with nothing. He had a plastic Provigo (supermarket) bag in his hand."

At the age of 62, Lévesque stepped down from the political stage to pursue a few more of life's pleasures. With a renewed sense of energy and excitement, Lévesque travelled around the world (the ticket was a parting gift from the PQ), wrote his memoirs, and returned briefly to radio journalism.

On November 1, 1987, Lévesque told his wife that he had indigestion. Corinne urged him to go to the hospital, but Lévesque was reluctant. He had a fear of doctors ever since his father died prematurely death following what should have been a routine operation.

Lévesque spent a quiet evening with Corinne at their Nun's Island home. They played Scrabble, one of Lévesque's favourite pastimes. With his last seven letters, Lévesque spelled "mondaine" (worldly). Shortly thereafter, he collapsed of a massive heart attack.

Corinne called an ambulance and gave Lévesque mouth-to-mouth resuscitation and chest massage. But when the ambulance paramedics arrived, Lévesque was already dead.

Most Quebeckers were devastated by the loss of this great man. Even Lévesque's political rivals acknowledged his significant impact on the evolution of Quebec society. René Lévesque was a man of integrity and a man of passion. He personified the modern province that he had helped to create. Quebeckers had a wild ride with René Lévesque during his lifetime — from delirious heights to devastating lows — and back again.

Now it was over. Lévesque was gone.

Bibliography

Desbarats, Peter. *René: A Canadian in Search of a Country*. Toronto: McClelland and Stewart, 1976.

Fraser, Graham. *René Lévesque and the Parti Québécois in Power*. Montréal: McGill-Queen's University Press, 2001.

Godin, Pierre. *René Lévesque, Un enfant de siècle (1922–1960)*. Montréal: Les Éditions du Boréal, 1994.

Godin, Pierre. *René Lévesque, Héros malgré lui (1960–1976)*. Montréal: Les Éditions du Boréal, 1997.

Godin, Pierre. *René Lévesque, L'espoir et le chagrin (1976–1980)*. Montréal: Les Éditions du Boréal, 2001.

Lévesque, René. *Memoirs*. Toronto: McClelland and Stewart, 1986. (Translation, English edition Philip Stratford) Published by arrangement with Editions Québec/Amérique.

Poulin, Margeurite. *René Lévesque: Une vie, une nation*. Montreal: XYZ Éditeur, 2003.

Thomson, Dale C. *Jean Lesage & the Quiet Revolution*. Toronto: Macmillan of Canada, 1984.

Audio Recording (a radio documentary)
Bouchard, Jacques. *Point de Mire sur René Lévesque*. Montreal: Radio-Canada/GSI Musique, 2002.

Acknowledgments

The author gratefully acknowledges John Durnford for contributing his personal perspective on the impact of René Lévesque on Quebec society.

Thanks also to Larry, Philippe, Nathalie, Nancy, and Gordon for their help minding Hugh and Charlotte.

About the Author

Megan Durnford is a freelance writer in Montréal. Her articles have been published in magazines and newspapers across the country. For more than a decade, Megan has also worked on multimedia projects about scientific and historical topics.

AMAZING STORIES™

CHRISTMAS IN QUEBEC

Heartwarming Legends, Tales, and Traditions

HOLIDAY

by Megan Durnford

CHRISTMAS IN QUEBEC
Heartwarming Legends, Tales, and Traditions

"Finally, one little girl piped up with the suggestion that they should call the fire department... Soon, a couple of fire engines arrived on the scene, and no less than six firemen helped Santa and his big bag down from the roof."

Christmas is a time for celebrating with friends and family and for sharing stories, memories, and good cheer. This compilation brings to life the very best holiday stories from across Quebec. From the early days of exploration to the modern day, and from heartwarming inspirational tales to dangerous escapades, this is a collection to treasure for many years to come.

 True stories. Truly Canadian.

ISBN 1-55153-784-2

AMAZING STORIES™

PIERRE ELLIOTT TRUDEAU

The Fascinating Life of Canada's Most Flamboyant Prime Minister

BIOGRAPHY
by Stan Sauerwein

PIERRE ELLIOTT TRUDEAU
The Fascinating Life of Canada's Most Flamboyant Prime Minister

"To a rapt national television audience, the soft-spoken minister with the Caesar-style haircut calmly justified his bill, saying, 'the State has no place in the bedrooms of the nation.'"

Pierre Trudeau was unlike any prime minister Canada had ever known or will ever see again. His unique style, charisma, bravado, and sharp wit galvanized a nation, creating the "Trudeaumania" that swept him into office. He was a man that Canadians either loved or hated.

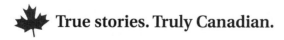 True stories. Truly Canadian.

ISBN 1-55153-945-4

AMAZING STORIES™

ÉTIENNE BRÛLÉ

The Mysterious Life and Times
of an Early Canadian Legend

HISTORY/BIOGRAPHY
by Gail Douglas

ÉTIENNE BRÛLÉ
Canada's Most Famous Revolutionary

"Brûlé was fully aware of the risks of heading into the heart of Iroquois territory.... At every step of the way he would be in danger of being captured, tortured, and killed. How could he resist?"

Étienne Brûlé was an enigma. But he was also a legend — even in his own time — as a scout and as a spy for Samuel de Champlain. Tales of his spectacular adventures, his outrageous behaviour, and his uncanny ability to be completely at home deep in the Canadian wilderness have endured for 400 years.

 True stories. Truly Canadian.

ISBN 1-55153-961-6

EARLY VOYAGEURS
The Incredible Adventures
of the Fearless Fur Traders

"The trips they undertake, the strains they endure, the dangers to which they are exposed, and... the efforts they have to make, all of this defies the imagination."
Francois-Xavier de Charlevoix, Missionary

For more than 200 years, voyageur canoes charged across the waters from Quebec to British Columbia, and north to Hudson Bay. Spending months at a time in the backwoods, braving dangerous rapids, and portaging over rough terrain, the voyageurs were the epitome of tough, rugged adventurers.

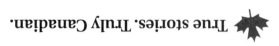 True stories. Truly Canadian.

ISBN 1-55153-970-5

OTHER AMAZING STORIES

ISBN	Title	ISBN	Title
1-55153-959-4	A War Bride's Story	1-55153-951-9	Ontario Murders
1-55153-794-X	Calgary Flames	1-55153-790-7	Ottawa Senators
1-55153-947-0	Canada's Rumrunners	1-55153-960-8	Ottawa Titans
1-55153-966-7	Canadian Spies	1-55153-945-4	Pierre Elliot Trudeau
1-55153-795-8	D-Day	1-55153-981-0	Rattenbury
1-55153-972-1	David Thompson	1-55153-991-8	Rebel Women
1-55153-982-9	Dinosaur Hunters	1-55153-995-0	Rescue Dogs
1-55153-970-5	Early Voyageurs	1-55153-985-3	Riding on the Wild Side
1-55153-798-2	Edmonton Oilers	1-55153-974-8	Risk Takers and Innovators
1-55153-968-3	Edwin Alonzo Boyd	1-55153-956-X	Robert Service
1-55153-996-9	Emily Carr	1-55153-799-0	Roberta Bondar
1-55153-961-6	Étienne Brûlé	1-55153-997-7	Sam Steele
1-55153-791-5	Extraordinary Accounts of Native Life on the West Coast	1-55153-954-3	Snowmobile Adventures
		1-55153-971-3	Stolen Horses
		1-55153-952-7	Strange Events
1-55153-993-4	Ghost Town Stories	1-55153-783-4	Strange Events and More
1-55153-992-6	Ghost Town Stories II	1-55153-986-1	Tales from the West Coast
1-55153-984-5	Ghost Town Stories III	1-55153-978-0	The Avro Arrow Story
1-55153-973-X	Great Canadian Love Stories	1-55153-943-8	The Black Donnellys
		1-55153-942-X	The Halifax Explosion
1-55153-777-X	Great Cat Stories	1-55153-994-2	The Heart of a Horse
1-55153-946-2	Great Dog Stories	1-55153-944-6	The Life of a Loyalist
1-55153-773-7	Great Military Leaders	1-55153-787-7	The Mad Trapper
1-55153-785-0	Grey Owl	1-55153-789-3	The Mounties
1-55153-958-6	Hudson's Bay Company Adventures	1-55153-948-9	The War of 1812 Against the States
1-55153-969-1	Klondike Joe Boyle	1-55153-788-5	Toronto Maple Leafs
1-55153-980-2	Legendary Show Jumpers	1-55153-976-4	Trailblazing Sports Heroes
1-55153-775-3	Lucy Maud Montgomery		
1-55153-967-5	Marie Anne Lagimodière	1-55153-977-2	Unsung Heroes of the Royal Canadian Air Force
1-55153-964-0	Marilyn Bell		
1-55153-999-3	Mary Schäffer	1-55153-792-3	Vancouver Canucks
1-55153-953-5	Moe Norman	1-55153-989-6	Vancouver's Old-Time Scoundrels
1-55153-965-9	Native Chiefs and Famous Métis		
		1-55153-990-X	West Coast Adventures
1-55153-962-4	Niagara Daredevils	1-55153-987-X	Wilderness Tales
1-55153-793-1	Norman Bethune	1-55153-873-3	Women Explorers

These titles are available wherever you buy books. If you have trouble finding the book you want, call the Altitude order desk at **1-800-957-6888**, e-mail your request to: **orderdesk@altitudepublishing.com** or visit our Web site **at www.amazingstories.ca**

New AMAZING STORIES titles are published every month.